Nick Vandome

iPhone
for Seniors

in
easy steps

for iPhone models with iOS 11
illustrated using iPhone 8 and iPhone 8 Plus

In easy steps is an imprint of In Easy Steps Limited
16 Hamilton Terrace · Holly Walk · Leamington Spa
Warwickshire · United Kingdom · CV32 4LY
www.ineasysteps.com

Notice of Liability
Every effort has been made to ensure that this book contains accurate
and current information. However, In Easy Steps Limited and the
author shall not be liable for any loss or damage suffered by readers
as a result of any information contained herein.

Trademarks
iPhone® is a registered trademark of Apple Computer, Inc. All other
trademarks are acknowledged as belonging to their respective
companies.

In Easy Steps Limited supports The Forest Stewardship Council (FSC),
the leading international forest certification organization. All our titles
that are printed on Greenpeace approved FSC certified paper carry the
FSC logo.

FSC
www.fsc.org

MIX
Paper from
responsible sources
FSC® C020837

Printed and bound in the United Kingdom

ISBN 978-1-84078-791-7

Contents

7 Hands on with Apps — 113

8 Apps for Every Day — 129

9 Relaxing with your iPhone — 141

1 Your New iPhone 8

The iPhone 8 is a sleek, stylish smartphone that is ideal for anyone, of any age. This chapter introduces the two models of the iPhone 8, and takes you through its buttons and controls. It also shows how to set it up ready for use, and access some of its features and settings to get started.

Hands on with the iPhone 8

The iPhone is one of the great success stories of the digital age. It is the world's leading smartphone: a touchscreen phone that can be used for not only making calls and sending text messages, but also for online access and a huge range of tasks through the use of apps (programs that come pre-installed, or can be downloaded from the online Apple App Store). Essentially, the iPhone is a powerful, compact computer that can be used for communication, entertainment, organization and most things in between.

The latest range of iPhones includes the iPhone X (see pages 10-11) and the iPhone 8, which is an update to the traditional range of iPhone models. The iPhone 8 comes in two sizes: the iPhone 8, which has a screen size of 4.7 inches (measured diagonally) and the iPhone 8 Plus, which has a screen size of 5.5 inches (measured diagonally). Apart from their sizes, both models have the same features, functionality and operating system (iOS 11). Some of the features on the front of the iPhone 8 include:

Don't forget

Although the iPhone X (see pages 10-11) is the latest flagship model of iPhone, the examples in the book use the more widely adopted iPhone 8. Both use the iOS 11 operating system, so most of the functionality is the same for all models.

Hot tip

Due to its larger screen size, the iPhone 8 Plus is capable of displaying the Home screen in both portrait and landscape mode.

NEW

The New icon pictured above indicates a new or enhanced feature introduced with the iPhone 8 or the latest version of its operating system, iOS 11.

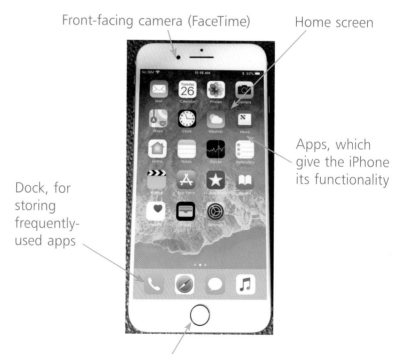

Front-facing camera (FaceTime)

Home screen

Apps, which give the iPhone its functionality

Dock, for storing frequently-used apps

Home button (can also serve as a Touch ID sensor)

What do you get?

The iPhone box contains all of the items required to use your new iPhone, charge it, and open the SIM tray to add a SIM card. The various components are:

- **iPhone 8 or 8 Plus**. The iPhone will be turned off, but there should be enough charge in the battery to turn it on without having to charge it first. Press on this button to turn on the iPhone.

- **The Lightning to USB cable**. This can be used for charging the iPhone, or connecting it to a computer for downloading items.

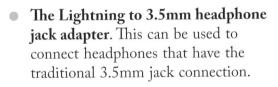

- **The EarPods**. These can be used to listen to audio items on your iPhone. They can also be used to manage phone calls using the central control button (see page 50 for details). There is no headphone jack for the iPhone 8 EarPods, as they connect via the Lightning connector.

- **The Lightning to 3.5mm headphone jack adapter**. This can be used to connect headphones that have the traditional 3.5mm jack connection.

- **The SIM tool**. This is a small metal gadget that is in a cardboard envelope in the iPhone box. It is used to open the SIM tray so that a SIM card can be inserted (see pages 14-15 for details).

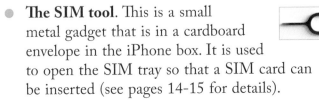

There is a wide range of accessories for the iPhone. These include cases in a range of colors and materials. These cases give some protection to the body of your iPhone.

To charge your iPhone with the Lightning to USB cable: insert the Lightning connector into the bottom of the iPhone, and insert the USB connector into the plug that is also provided in the iPhone box. Connect the plug to a socket to charge your iPhone.

The iPhone 8 and 8 Plus support wireless charging, by placing the device on a base station.

The iPhone X is a new product in Apple's iPhone range.

Beware

The innovation in the iPhone X does not come cheap. The standard model is $999 in the US and an equivalent £999 in the UK.

Don't forget

Support for Augmented Reality (AR) is also provided with the iPhone X. This is the process of incorporating animations or graphical elements into real-life scenes being viewed by the iPhone X. Apple has provided a range of new tools to AR developers, and this is undoubtedly an area that will expand considerably in the near future.

Introducing iPhone X

Just as the original iPhone helped to redefine the way we use phones and heralded the era of the smartphone, so Apple's latest model of iPhone, the iPhone X (pronounced "ten") aims to move the evolution of the smartphone to the next level of design and functionality.

The iPhone X celebrates the 10th anniversary of the launch of the iPhone, and introduces a range of features that will doubtless become the standard for smartphones for years to come. It is likely that several of these features will be part of the next range of iPhones.

All-glass design

The first thing that is noticeable about the iPhone X is its stunning, all-glass display. This is piece of glass that surrounds the iPhone X and produces the best quality screen yet for an iPhone with the 5.8 inch (measured diagonally) Super Retina HD True Tone Display.

No Home button

The main functionality difference between the iPhone X and the other iPhone models is that there is no Home button. What was previously used to unlock the iPhone and access a range of features has been replaced with a range of swiping gestures. For instance, to get to the Home screen at any point, swipe up from the bottom of the screen. Although the lack of a Home button may take a bit of getting used to initially, it is a way of removing a moving part and an area where dust and water can penetrate. It also contributes to the ability for the screen to cover more of the phone's area, so that more of it can be used to view content. The Touch ID functionality that was previously accessed through the Home button has been replaced by face recognition technology for unlocking the iPhone X.

Face ID

Face ID is the face recognition system used on the iPhone X to unlock the phone. This was previously done using the fingerprint Touch ID and the Home button. Face ID operates using a range of sensors and cameras contained in the notch at the top of the iPhone X. Once a face has been recognized,

it can be used to unlock the phone in different lighting conditions and also in the dark, using infrared sensors. Face ID can also recognize if you have changed your appearance through adding a hat, glasses or changing your hairstyle. Once Face ID has been set up, unlock your iPhone X simply by looking at it and swiping up on the Home screen.

Accessing items

Because there is no Home button, some items that have previously been accessed from here now have different ways of being accessed:

- **Control Center**. The Control Center has been redesigned with iOS 11, and on the iPhone X it is accessed by swiping down from the right-hand corner of the top of the phone.

- **Notification Center**. The Notification Center is accessed by swiping down from the left-hand corner of the top of the phone, as opposed to swiping down from the middle, as on previous iPhones.

- **App Switcher**. The App Switcher was previously accessed by double-pressing on the Home button. On the iPhone X this is done by swiping up from the bottom of the screen, in the same way as accessing the Home screen, and pressing briefly on the Home screen.

- **Siri**. The digital voice assistant, Siri, is accessed by using the "Hey Siri" functionality, or by pressing the side button (on the right-hand edge) for a couple of seconds.

It is claimed Face ID improves security in terms of someone else being able to unlock a phone with Face ID. With Touch ID there was a 1:50,000 chance of someone else being able to unlock an iPhone; with Face ID on the iPhone X it is 1:1,000,000.

The iPhone X also supports animated emojis, known as animojis. These are emojis that use face-tracking technology (using the same cameras as for Face ID) to superimpose your facial expressions onto a graphical emoji.

11

iPhone 8 Nuts and Bolts

Don't forget

For more details on turning on the iPhone, see page 17.

Don't forget

The iPhone 8 and 8 Plus come in Gold, Silver and Space Gray.

Don't forget

To make phone calls with your iPhone you need to have an active SIM card inserted, and a suitable service provider for cellular (mobile) calls and data. The iPhone 8 uses a nano SIM card, which is smaller than both the standard size and the micro size.

On/Off button

The button for turning the iPhone On and Off (and putting it into Sleep mode) is located on the top right-hand side of the body (looking at the screen). As with other buttons on the body, it is slightly raised, to make it easier to locate just by touch.

Volume controls

Volume is controlled using two separate buttons on the left-hand side of the body. They do not have symbols on them but they are used to increase and decrease the volume.

Ringer/silent (use this to turn the ringer on or off for when a call or a notification is received)

Volume up

Volume down

The Nano SIM Tray

The iPhone 8 uses a nano SIM (smaller than the micro SIM used in some older iPhone models).

Push the SIM tool firmly into this hole to access the SIM tray and insert a SIM card (see pages 14-15 for details)

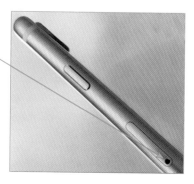

Lightning connector, speakers and microphone

These are located at the bottom of the iPhone.

Stereo speakers

Microphone   Lightning connector

Back view of the iPhone 8

This contains the main camera, the LED flash and the rear microphone.

Rear microphone   LED flash (and torch)

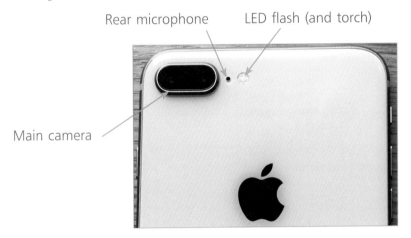

Main camera

The main camera is a high-quality 12-megapixel camera. It can capture excellent photos and also 4K (ultra-high definition) and high definition (HD) video. The iSight camera on the iPhone 8 Plus also comes with a wide-angle and telephoto lens capability. The front-facing FaceTime camera (see page 8) has a lower resolution (7 megapixels) and although it can also be used for photos and videos, it is best used for video calls using the FaceTime app (see pages 110-111). It can also be used for taking "selfies"; the modern craze of taking a photo of yourself and then posting it online on a social media site such as Facebook.

The iPhone 8 Plus has two lenses for the iSight camera; one wide-angle and one telephoto. They combine to take each shot

Don't forget

The phone services for the iPhone are provided by companies that enable access to their mobile networks, which you will be able to use for phone calls, texts and mobile data for access to the internet. Companies provide different packages: you can buy the iPhone for a reduced sum and then pay a monthly contract, typically for 12 or 24 months. Despite the fact that the iPhone will be cheaper, this works out more expensive over the period of the contract. Another option is to buy the iPhone (make sure it is unlocked so that you can use any SIM card) and use a SIM-only offer. This way, you can buy a package that suits you for calls, texts and mobile data. Look for offers that have unlimited data for internet access.

Inserting the SIM

The SIM card for the iPhone 8 will be provided by your mobile carrier; i.e. the company that provides your cellular phone and data services. Without this, you would still be able to communicate with your iPhone, but only via Wi-Fi and compatible services. A SIM card gives you access to a mobile network too. Some iPhones come with the SIM pre-installed, but you can also insert one yourself. To do this:

1 Take the SIM tool out of the iPhone box and remove it from its cardboard packaging

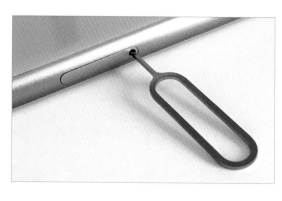

2 Insert the SIM tool into the small hole on the SIM slot on the side of the iPhone 8, as shown on page 12

3 Press the tool firmly into the hole so that the SIM tray pops out and

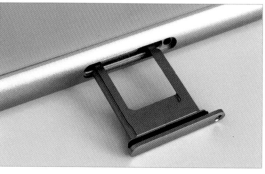

starts to appear. Pull the SIM tray fully out

4 Place the SIM card with the metal contacts face downwards. Place the SIM tray in position so that the diagonal cut is in the same position as the cut on the SIM card

Hot tip

If you lose the SIM tool you can use the end of a stretched-out paper clip instead.

5 Place the SIM card into the SIM tray. It should fit flush, resting on a narrow ridge underneath it, with the diagonal cut on the card matching the cut in the tray

Beware

The SIM tray can only be inserted in one way. If it appears to encounter resistance, do not force it; take it out and try again. The hole in the SIM tray should be nearest to the bottom of the phone body.

6 Place your thumb over the bottom of the SIM tray, covering the SIM card, and place the tray into the SIM slot, with the metal contacts facing the back of the phone. Push the tray firmly into the slot until it clicks into place

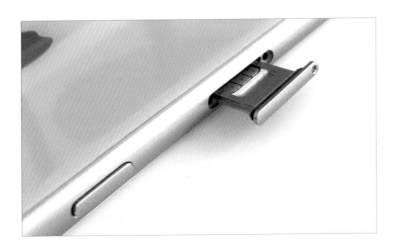

15

The amount of storage you need may change once you have bought your iPhone. If possible, buy a version with as much storage as your budget allows.

Don't forget

3G and 4G refer to the data speeds for mobile connections. The G stands for Generation. 4G is faster than 3G and is becoming more widely available from mobile network providers.

Hot tip

To connect your iPhone to an HDTV you will need an Apple Lightning (or Dock) Digital AV Adapter or an Apple Lightning (or Dock) to VGA Adapter (sold separately).

iPhone Specifications

Apart from their sizes, the iPhone 8 and iPhone 8 Plus models have almost identical specifications:

- **Processor**: This determines the speed at which the iPhone 8 operates and how quickly tasks are performed. Both models have a fast A11 Bionic chip processor.

- **Screen**: The iPhone 8 has a 4.7 inch screen, and for the iPhone 8 Plus it is 5.5 inches. Both are Retina HD True Tone quality, which gives a very clear, sharp image.

- **Storage**: This determines how much content you can store on your iPhone. For the iPhone 8 and 8 Plus, the storage capacity is either 64GB or 256GB.

- **Connectivity**: The options for this are Wi-Fi (support for fast 802.11ac Wi-Fi) and 3G/4G connectivity for calls and the internet, and Bluetooth 5.0 for connecting to devices over short distances.

- **Operating system**: Both the iPhone 8 and the iPhone 8 Plus run on the iOS 11 operating system.

- **Battery power**: The iPhone 8 provides up to 40 hours of wireless audio playback, 13 hours' video playback, and 14 hours' talk time on 3G. The iPhone 8 Plus provides 60 hours for wireless audio, 14 for video and 21 hours' talk time. Web use over Wi-Fi is up to 12 and 13 hours respectively for the iPhone 8 and iPhone 8 Plus, with both slightly lower over 3G/4G.

- **Input/Output**: These are a Lightning connector port (for charging, headphones and connecting to a computer), built-in speaker and a built-in microphone (the iPhone 8 does not have a separate headphone jack).

- **Sensors**: The sensors are: accelerometer, barometer, ambient light sensor, proximity sensor and gyroscope.

- **TV and video**: This connects your iPhone to a High Definition TV with AirPlay Mirroring, which mirrors what's on your iPhone, wirelessly via Apple TV.

Turning On

The first thing you will want to do with your iPhone is to turn it on. To do this:

1 Press and hold on the **On/Off** button for a few seconds. Keep it pressed until the Apple icon appears

2 After a few seconds the iPhone will power on, displaying the Lock screen. Press the **Home** button to access the Home screen

Hot tip

If your iPhone ever freezes, or if something is not working properly, it can be rebooted by holding down the **Home** button and the **On/Off** button for 10 seconds, and then turning it on again by pressing and holding the **On/Off** button.

Hot tip

Buy a glass screen protector to help preserve your iPhone's screen. This will help prevent marks and scratches, and can also save the screen if it is broken: the protector breaks rather than the iPhone's screen itself.

Turning Off and Sleep

Whenever the iPhone is not in use, it is a good idea to put it to sleep, or turn it off, to save power. If you will be using it again shortly then Sleep is the best option, but if you are not going to be using the phone for a longer period, e.g. overnight, then it may be best to turn it off.

To put the iPhone to sleep:

Don't forget

In Sleep mode (also known as Standby) the iPhone 8 will retain battery power for up to 10 days (240 hours). For the iPhone 8 Plus this is 16 days (384 hours).

1 Press the **On/Off** button once to put the iPhone to sleep and activate the Lock screen

To turn the iPhone off:

Don't forget

You will need an Apple ID for all Apple online services. This is free – to register go to https://appleid.apple. com

Tap on **Create Your Apple ID**. You will be prompted to enter your email address and a password. Then follow the simple on-screen instructions, including agreeing to their terms. Tap on Create Apple ID when ready.

1 Press and hold the **On/Off** button until the Power Off screen appears. Swipe the **slide to power off** button to the right to turn off the iPhone

Getting Set Up

When you first turn on your iPhone 8, there will be a series of setup screens. These include the following options (which can also be accessed from the **Settings** app):

- **Language**. Select the language you want to use.

- **Country**. Select the country in which you are located.

- **Quick Start**. This can be used to transfer settings from another compatible iOS device.

- **Wi-Fi network**. Connect to the internet, using either your own home network or a public Wi-Fi hotspot.

- **Touch ID.** Use this on compatible models to create a Touch ID for unlocking your iPhone, with a fingerprint.

- **Create Passcode**. This can be used to create a numerical passcode for unlocking your iPhone.

- **Apps and Data (iCloud, iTunes, or new)**. This can be used to set up your iPhone using an existing iCloud or iTunes backup, or as a new device.

- **Apple ID and iCloud**. An Apple ID can be used to create an iCloud account for backing up content and using iTunes, the App Store, Messages and iBooks.

- **Location Services**. This determines whether your iPhone can use your geographical location for apps.

- **Siri.** This can be used to set up Siri, the digital voice assistant, ready for use.

- **iPhone Analytics**. This allows details about your iPhone and its apps to be sent to Apple and developers.

- **True Tone Display**. This can be used to allow the screen to adapt to ambient lighting conditions.

- **Customize the Home button**. Use this to select the amount of pressure used on the Home button.

- **Display Zoom**. Change the size of the display icons.

The iPhone offers several features for users who have difficulty with hearing, vision, physical or motor skills. These are covered on pages 178-181.

For more information about using iCloud, see Chapter 3.

The Find My iPhone function can also be set up within the **iCloud** section of the **Settings** app (see pages 184-185).

The Cellular (Mobile Data) settings contain the **Data Roaming** option (**Cellular > Cellular Data Options**): if you are traveling abroad you may want to turn this **Off** to avoid undue charges for when you are connected to the internet. If in doubt, contact your provider before you go.

To change the iPhone's wallpaper, tap once on the **Choose a New Wallpaper** option in the **Wallpaper** setting. From here, you can select system images, or ones that you have taken yourself and saved on your iPhone.

iPhone Settings

The Settings app controls settings for the way the iPhone and its apps operate:

- **Apple ID, iCloud, iTunes & App Store**. Contains settings for these items.

- **Airplane Mode**. This can be used to disable network connectivity while on an airplane.

- **Wi-Fi**. This enables you to select a wireless network.

- **Bluetooth**. Turn this On to connect Bluetooth devices.

- **Cellular (Mobile Data)**. These are the settings that will be used with your cellular (mobile) service provider.

- **Personal Hotspot**. This can be used to share your internet connection.

- **Carrier**. This can be used to locate relevant signals from cellular carriers. By default, it is On for Automatic.

- **Notifications**. This determines how the Notification Center operates (see pages 26-27).

- **Control Center**. This determines how the Control Center operates (see pages 34-37).

- **Do Not Disturb**. Use this to specify times when you do not want to receive audio alerts or FaceTime video calls.

- **General**. This contains a range of common settings.

- **Display & Brightness**. This can be used to set the screen brightness, text size and bold text.

- **Wallpaper**. This can be used to select a wallpaper.

- **Sounds & Haptics**. This has options for setting sounds for alerts and physical haptic feedback from keys.

- **Siri & Search**. Options for the digital voice assistant.

- **Touch ID & Passcode**. This has options for adding a passcode or fingerprint ID for unlocking the iPhone.

- **Emergency SOS.** This can be used to set an Auto Call emergency number (by pressing the sleep/wake button five times in quick succession).

- **Battery**. This can be used to view battery usage by apps.

- **Privacy**. This can be used to activate Location Services so that your location can be used by specific apps.

- **iTunes & App Store**. This can be used to specify downloading options for the iTunes and App Stores.

- **Wallet & Apple Pay**. This can be used to add credit or debit cards for use with Apple Pay (see pages 48-49).

- **Accounts & Passwords.** This contains options for managing website passwords and adding online accounts.

- **Mail, Contacts, Calendars**. These are three separate settings that have options for how these apps operate.

- **Notes**. This has formatting options for the Notes app.

- **Reminders**. This has an option for syncing your reminders for other devices, covering a period of time.

- **Phone**. Settings for making calls (see page 74).

- **Messages**. Options for how the Messages app operates.

- **FaceTime**. This is used to turn video calling On or Off.

- **Maps**. This has options for map distances and map type.

- **Compass**. One setting, to use True North or not.

- **Safari**. Settings for the default iPhone web browser.

- **News**. Settings for specifying access for the News app.

- **Camera**. This has options for the camera's operation.

- **Photos**. This has options for sharing photos via iCloud.

- **Music, Videos, iBooks**, and **Podcasts**. Settings for how these four apps manage and display content.

If a Settings option has an On/Off button next to it, this can be changed by swiping the button to either the left or right. Green indicates that the option is **On**. Select **Settings** > **General** > **Accessibility** > **On/Off Labels** to show or hide the icons on each button.

Tap on a link to see additional options:

Tap once here to move back to the previous page for the selected setting:

iOS 11 is a new feature introduced with the iPhone 8.

About iOS 11

iOS 11 is the latest version of the operating system for Apple's mobile devices, including the iPhone and also the iPad and the iPod Touch.

iOS 11 further enhances the user experience for which the mobile operating system is renowned. This includes:

- The redesigned Control Center. This has an updated layout and is also customizable so that you can select specific items to appear in the Control Center.

- The redesigned App Store, to make it easier to find and download the apps you want.

- The Messages app has been enhanced, so that it is easier to access the app drawer, for adding a variety of content to text messages.

- Siri, the digital voice assistant, has been enhanced, with more expressive voice options, a greater capacity for providing suggestions in a range of apps, and also a translation option.

- The keyboard now has a one-handed option, whereby the keyboard moves to either the left-hand, or right-hand, side of the screen, to enable one-handed typing with the other hand.

- The camera has an increased range of filters that can be applied with taking a photo.

- Live Photos (the short, animated, movies that can be created with the camera) have been enhanced, to include new effects, such as looping a photo and creating a long exposure.

- The new Files app, which can be used for organizing and accessing documents, including those held in separate online storage services such as Dropbox and Google Drive. Items in the Files app are stored within the iCloud Drive, which can be managed within Settings.

To check the version of the iOS, look in **Settings** > **General** > **Software Update**.

Using the Lock Screen

To save power, it is possible to set your iPhone screen to auto-lock. This is the equivalent of the Sleep option on a traditional computer. To do this:

1 Tap once on the **Settings** app

2 Tap once on the **Display & Brightness** tab

3 Tap once on the **Auto-Lock** link

Auto-Lock	Never >

4 Tap once on the time of non-use after which you wish the screen to be locked

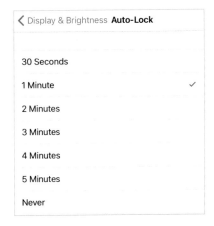

‹ Display & Brightness **Auto-Lock**

30 Seconds

1 Minute ✓

2 Minutes

3 Minutes

4 Minutes

5 Minutes

Never

5 Once the screen is locked, press the **Home** button to unlock the screen

Touch ID and Passcode

Adding a passcode

When the iPhone is locked, i.e. the Lock screen is displayed, it can be unlocked simply by pressing the **Home** button. However, this is not secure, as anyone could unlock the phone. A more secure option is to add a numerical passcode. To do this:

Beware

If you use a passcode to lock your iPhone write it down, but store it in a location away from the iPhone.

Don't forget

Tap once on the **Passcode Options** link in Step 3 to access other options for creating a passcode. These include a **Custom Alphanumeric Code**, a **Custom Numeric Code** and a **4-Digit Code**. The 4-Digit Code is the least secure and the Alphanumeric Code is the most secure, as it can use a combination of numbers, letters and symbols.

1 Select **Settings > Touch ID & Passcode**

Touch ID & Passcode

2 Tap once on the **Turn Passcode On** button

< Settings   **Passcode Lock**

Turn Passcode On

Change Passcode

Require Passcode   Immediately >

3 Enter a six-digit passcode. This can be used to unlock your iPhone from the Lock screen

Set Passcode   Cancel

Enter a passcode

● ● ● ● ○ ○

Passcode Options

1	2 ABC	3 DEF
4 GHI	5 JKL	6 MNO
7 PQRS	8 TUV	9 WXYZ
	0	⌫

4 Once a passcode

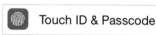
Require Passcode   Immediately >

has been created, tap once on the **Require Passcode** button in Step 2 to specify a time period until the passcode is required on the Lock screen. The best option is **Immediately**, otherwise someone else could access your iPhone

Fingerprint sensor with Touch ID

For greater security, the **Home** button can be used as a fingerprint sensor to unlock your iPhone with the fingerprint that has set it up. (A passcode also has to be set up in case the Touch ID does not work.) To do this:

1 Select **Settings** > **Touch ID & Passcode**

2 Create a passcode as shown opposite (this is required if the fingerprint sensor is unavailable for any reason)

3 Drag the **iPhone Unlock** button to **On** and tap once on the **Add a Fingerprint...** link. This presents a screen for creating your Touch ID

4 Place your finger on the **Home** button several times until the Touch ID is created. This will include capturing the edges of your finger. The screens move automatically after each part is captured and the fingerprint icon turns red

Hot tip

Touch ID can also be used for contactless purchases for Apple Pay (see pages 48-49) and purchases in the iTunes and App Stores. Drag the buttons **On** in Step 3 if you want to use these functions. If these are activated then purchases can be made by pressing the **Home** button with your unique Touch ID.

Don't forget

The fingerprint sensor is very effective, although it may take a bit of practice until you can get the right position for your finger to unlock the iPhone, first time, every time. It can only be unlocked with the same finger that created the Touch ID in Step 4, although more than one fingerprint can be added.

Notifications

Notifications can be used with iOS 11 so that you never miss an important message or update. Notifications can be viewed in the Notification Center and also on the Lock screen. To set up and use Notifications:

The Notification Center can be accessed by dragging down from the top of the screen, in any app.

Drag the **Show on Lock Screen** to **On** in Step 4 to enable notifications for the selected app to be displayed even when the iPhone is locked.

Hot tip

Text messages can be replied to directly from the Lock screen, without unlocking the iPhone. To do this, press on the message on the Lock screen and compose a reply as normal.

26

1. Tap once on the **Settings** app

2. Tap once on the **Notifications** tab

3. Under **Notification Style**, tap once on an item to select the notification settings for a specific app

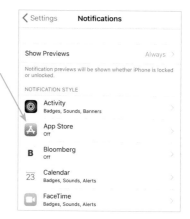

4. Drag the **Allow Notifications** button to **On** to display notifications from this app in the Notification Center

5. Tap here to select the style for how the notification appears

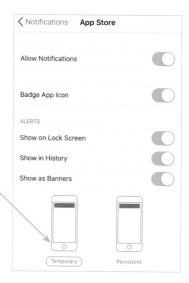

6 Swipe down from the top of the iPhone screen, from the Home screen or any app, to view your notifications in the Notification Center. This is split into two sections: the Today section, which contains widgets with real-time information about topics such as the weather, stocks and news and the Up Next calendar item; and notifications from the apps selected in Step 3 opposite (swipe from right to left on the Today section to access this)

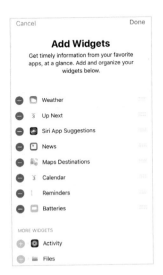

Don't forget

The items in Step 6 can also be viewed directly on the Lock screen. Swipe left and right to view the two separate screens. The Today section can also be viewed from the Home screen by swiping from left to right.

27

7 Swipe to the bottom of the Today section, and tap once on the **Edit** button to manage the widgets that appear here. Tap on a red circle to delete a widget from the Today page, or scroll down and tap on a green button to add a new widget

Hot tip

The Notification Center Today page can also be accessed by swiping from left to right on the main Home screen. Both pages can also be accessed by swiping down from the top of the Lock screen.

Updating Software

The operating system that powers the iPhone is known as iOS. This is a mobile computing operating system, and it is also used on the iPad and the iPod Touch. The latest version is iOS 11. Periodically, there are updates to the iOS to fix bugs and add new features. These can be downloaded to your iPhone once they are released:

Hot tip

It is always worth updating the iOS to keep up-to-date with fixes. Also, app developers update their products to use the latest iOS features.

Don't forget

The iOS software can also be updated via iTunes on a Mac or a PC if there isn't enough space on your iPhone. Connect the iPhone to the computer with the Lightning/USB cable. Open **iTunes** and click on this button on the top toolbar, click on the **Summary** tab, and click on the **Check for Update** button in the iPhone section.

1 Tap once on the **Settings** app

2 Tap once on the **General** tab
(A red tag indicates that an update is available)

3 Tap once on the **Software Update** link

4 If there is an update available it will be displayed here, with details of what is contained within it

5 Tap once on the **Download and Install** button to start the downloading process. The iOS update will then be done automatically

2 Starting to use your iPhone 8

This chapter covers the functions on the iPhone that you need to use it confidently and make the most of its features. From opening and closing apps to using Apple Pay, it explains the iPhone environment so you can quickly get up and running with it.

Home Button

The **Home** button, located at the bottom-middle of the iPhone, can be used to perform a number of tasks:

Hot tip

The **Home** button can also be used as a fingerprint sensor to set up Touch ID for unlocking the iPhone. See pages 24-25 for details.

1 Click once on the **Home** button to return to the Home screen at any point

2 Double-click on the **Home** button to access the **App Switcher** window. This shows the most recently-used and open apps

3 Press and hold on the **Home** button to access the Siri voice assistant function (see pages 38-41)

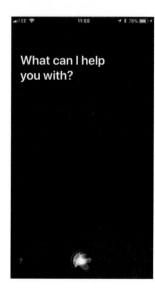

Opening and Closing Items

All apps on your iPhone can be opened with the minimum of fuss and effort:

1 Tap once on an icon to open the app

2 The app opens at its Home screen

3 Click once on the **Home** button to return to the iPhone Home screen

4 From the App Switcher window (see opposite) swipe left and right between open apps, and tap on one to make it the active app. Swipe an app to the top of the window in the App Switcher to close it

Don't forget

When you switch from one app to another, the first one stays open in the background. You can go back to it by accessing it from the App Switcher window or the Home screen.

Don't forget

To reopen an app that has been closed, click once on the **Home** button to go back to the Home screen and tap once on the app's icon here.

Using the Dock

By default, there are four apps on the Dock at the bottom of the iPhone's screen. These are the four that Apple thinks you will use most frequently:

- **Phone**, for making and receiving calls.

- **Safari**, for web browsing.

- **Messages**, for text messaging.

- **Music**.

You can rearrange the order in which the Dock apps appear:

1 Press and hold on one of the Dock apps until it starts to jiggle

2 Drag the app into its new position

3 Click once on the **Home** button to return from edit mode

With iOS 11, some of the pre-installed apps can be deleted from your iPhone. These are indicated by a cross in the top left-hand corner when you press on an app, as in Step 1.

Hot tip

Just above the Dock is a line of small white dots. These indicate how many screens of content there are on the iPhone. Tap on one of the dots to go to that screen.

Adding and removing Dock apps

You can also remove apps from the Dock and add new ones:

1 To remove an app from the Dock, press and hold it, and drag it onto the main screen area

2 To add an app to the Dock, press and hold it, and drag it onto the Dock

3 The number of items that can be added to the Dock is restricted to a maximum of four, as the icons do not resize

4 Click once on the **Home** button to return from edit mode

Don't forget

If items are removed from the Dock they are still available in the same way from the main screen. (When the iPhone 8 Plus is using landscape mode, the Dock appears down the right-hand side of the screen.)

The Control Center cannot be disabled from being accessed from the Home screen.

Don't forget

AirDrop is the functionality for sharing items wirelessly between compatible devices. Tap once on the **AirDrop** button in the Control Center and specify whether you want to share with **Contacts Only** or **Everyone**. Once AirDrop is set up, you can use the **Share** button in compatible apps to share items, such as photos, with any other AirDrop users in the vicinity.

Using the Control Center

The Control Center is a panel containing some of the most commonly-used options within the **Settings** app.

Accessing the Control Center

The Control Center can be accessed with one swipe from any screen within iOS 11, and it can also be accessed from the Lock screen. To set this up:

1 Tap once on the **Settings** app

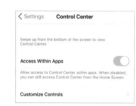

2 Tap once on the **Control Center** tab, and drag the **Access Within Apps** button On or Off to specify if the Control Center can be accessed from there (if it is Off, it can still be accessed from any Home screen)

3 Swipe up from the bottom of any screen to access the Control Center

Control Center functionality

The Control Panel contains items that have differing format and functionality. To access these:

1 Press and hold on the folder of four icons to access the **Airplane Mode**, **Cellular Data**, **Wi-Fi**, **Bluetooth**, **AirDrop** and **Personal Hotspot** options

2 Press on the **Music** button to expand the options for music controls, including playing or pausing items and changing the volume. Tap once on this icon to send music from your iPhone to other compatible devices, such as AirPod headphones or HomePods, Apple's wireless speakers

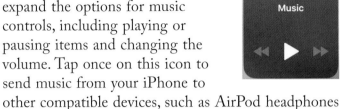

The Control Center has been enhanced in iOS 11.

3 Tap once on individual buttons to turn items On or Off (they change color depending on their state)

4 Drag on these items to increase or decrease the screen brightness and the volume

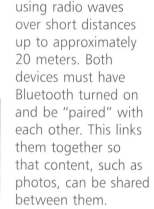

Hot tip

Bluetooth can be used to connect to other compatible devices, using radio waves over short distances up to approximately 20 meters. Both devices must have Bluetooth turned on and be "paired" with each other. This links them together so that content, such as photos, can be shared between them.

Don't forget

Press and hold on the Camera button to access options for taking a "selfie" (a self-portrait), recording a video, recording a slow-motion video and taking a standard photo.

...cont'd

Control Center controls

Access the items in the Control Center as follows:

- Tap once on this button to turn **Airplane mode** On or Off, for network connections.

- Tap once on this button to turn **Cellular Data** On or Off, for cellular networks.

- Tap once on this button to turn **Wi-Fi** On or Off.

- Tap once on this button to turn **Bluetooth** On or Off.

- Tap once on this button to activate **AirDrop** for sharing items with other AirDrop users.

- Tap once on this button to turn **Personal Hotspot** On or Off, to use your iPhone as a hotspot for connecting to the internet.

- Tap once on this button to **Lock** or **Unlock** screen rotation. If it is locked, the screen will not change when you change the orientation.

- Tap once on this button to turn **Do Not Disturb** mode On or Off.

- Tap once on this button to turn on the **Flashlight**. Press on the button to change the intensity of the flashlight.

- Tap once on this button to access the **Clock**, including a stopwatch and timer. Press on the button to access a scale for creating reminders.

- Tap once on this button to open the **Calculator** app.

- Tap once on this button to open the **Camera** app.

...cont'd

Customizing the Control Center

The items in the Control Center can be customized so that items can be added or removed. To do this:

1 Tap once on the **Settings** app

2 Tap once on the **Control Center** tab

3 Tap once on the **Customize Controls** button

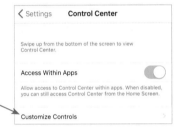

Customization of the Control Center is a new feature in iOS 11.

4 The items currently in the Control Center are shown at the top of the window; those that can be added are below them. Tap once on a red icon to remove an existing item, or tap once on a green icon to add new items to the Control Center

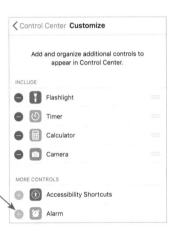

5 Items that are added in Step 4 are included in the Control Center, and can be accessed from here

Setting up Siri

Siri is the iPhone voice assistant that provides answers to a variety of verbal questions by looking at content in your iPhone and also web services. You can ask Siri questions relating to the apps on your iPhone, and also general questions such as weather conditions around the world, or sports results. Initially, Siri can be set up within the **Settings** app:

1 Tap once on the **Settings** app

2 Tap once on the **Siri & Search** tab

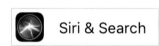

Options for Siri

Within the Siri setting there are options for its operation:

Siri can be used to translate English words or phrases into French, German, Italian, Mandarin Chinese and Spanish. This is a new feature in iOS 11.

38

1 Drag the **Listen for "Hey Siri"** button to **On** if you want to be able to access Siri just by saying **Hey Siri**

2 Make selections here for the language, voice type, feedback and your own details to use with Siri

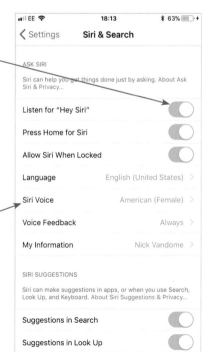

3 If using "Hey Siri", it has to be set up by training it for your voice. Tap once on the **Continue** button

Set Up "Hey Siri"

This helps Siri recognize your voice when you say "Hey Siri."

Continue

4 Repeat the range of phrases to train Siri to your voice. This is a five-step process

Say "Hey Siri" into the iPhone

5 Tap once on the **Done** button to complete the "Hey Siri" setup

"Hey Siri" Is Ready

Siri will recognize your voice whenever you say, "Hey Siri."

Done

Accessing Siri

There are two ways to access Siri (in addition to "Hey Siri"):

1 Press and hold the **Home** button until the Siri screen appears

2 Ask your question to Siri. After the reply, tap once on this icon to ask another question

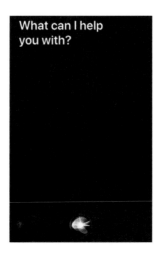

What can I help you with?

Siri can be used to open any of the pre-installed iPhone apps, simply by saying, for example, **Open Photos**.

Finding Things with Siri

Siri is very versatile and can be used for a wide range of functions, including finding things on your iPhone, searching the web, getting weather forecasts, finding locations, and even playing music.

Accessing your apps
To use Siri to find things on your iPhone:

Hot tip

Siri can also display specific contacts. Say, **Show me...** followed by the person's name to view their details (if they are in your contacts).

1 Access Siri as shown on page 39

2 To find something from your iPhone apps, ask a question such as **Open my contacts**

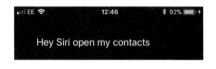

Hot tip

Siri can also read out your information: open an item such as calendar appointments and then say, **Read appointment**.

3 The requested app is displayed

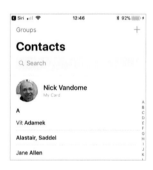

Getting the weather
You can ask Siri for weather forecasts for locations around the world. Simply ask for the weather in a certain city or location.

Don't forget

You can ask for weather forecasts for specific periods, such as **Today** or **This Week**. However, Siri's power of forecasting only stretches to 10 days in the future.

Finding locations

Siri is also effective for viewing locations within the Maps app. This can be done on an international, national or city level. Siri can also be used to get directions.

Searching locally

If Location Services is turned on for Siri, then you can ask for local information, such as **Show the nearest Indian restaurants**.

Hot tip

Siri in iOS 11 can be used with certain third-party apps to perform tasks such as booking a taxi or a restaurant table.

41

Playing music

You can use Siri to play any of the music that you have in the Music app. Simply ask Siri to play a track and it will start playing. (Music can be downloaded from the iTunes Store app; see page 144 for more details.)

Don't forget

Siri can also play a whole album as well as individual tracks. Ask for the album name to be played, and Siri should oblige.

To stop a song, simply say **Stop playing** and the song will be paused.

Searching with Spotlight

Siri can be used to search for items on your iPhone and you can also use the built-in search engine, Spotlight. To do this:

1 Swipe downwards from the center of the Home screen. This also activates the keyboard. Enter the search keywords into the Search box at the top of the window, and results will display automatically

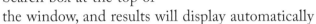

2 As keywords are entered into the Spotlight Search box, the options are shown underneath. The options become more defined as more words are entered

3 Results can be displayed for people and also items such as nearby attractions or restaurants. Any matches will appear at the top of the Spotlight window. Tap once on a result to view its details and its location in Maps (if applicable)

4 Swipe to the bottom of the Spotlight window to use the **Search Web**, **Search App Store** and **Search Maps** options for the required item

Don't forget

To return to the Home screen from the Spotlight Search page, press once on the **Home** button.

Hot tip

Enter the name of an app into the Spotlight Search box, and tap on the result to launch the app from here.

Navigating Around

The iPhone screen is very receptive to touch and this is the main method of navigating around, through a combination of swiping, tapping and pinching.

Swiping between Home screens

Once you have added more apps to your iPhone, they will start to fill up more Home screens. To move between these:

1 Swipe left or right with one or two fingers to move between Home screens

In addition to swiping between two screens there are a combination of tapping, swiping and pinching gestures that can be used to view items such as web pages, photos, maps and documents, and also to navigate around the iPhone.

Swiping up and down

Swipe up and down with one finger to move up or down web pages, photos, maps or documents. The content moves in the opposite direction of the swipe; i.e. if you swipe up, the page will move down, and vice versa.

Tapping and zooming

Double-tap with one finger to zoom in on a web page, photo, map or document. Double-tap with one finger to return to the original view.

Pinching and swiping

Swipe outwards with thumb and forefinger to zoom in on a web page, photo, map or document.

Pinch together with thumb and forefinger to zoom back out on a web page, photo, map or document.

You can also move between different screens by tapping once on the small white dots in the middle of the screen above the Dock.

You can also return to the first Home screen by clicking once on the **Home** button.

The faster you swipe on the screen, the faster the screen moves up or down.

Swiping outwards with thumb and forefinger enables you to zoom in on an item to a greater degree than double-tapping with one finger.

Reachability

Because of the size of both the iPhone 8 and iPhone 8 Plus, it is not always easy to access all items with one hand. This is overcome by a feature known as Reachability. This moves the items on the screen to the bottom half, and they can all be accessed from here.

The Reachability feature can be accessed from any screen of the iPhone.

1 By default, all items on the screen take up the whole area

2 Gently double-tap on the **Home** button (this is not the same as double-clicking the **Home** button, which activates the App Switcher screen)

3 The items on the top half of the screen are moved to the bottom half

4 The Reachability effect stays in place for one action; e.g. after you tap on an item, the screen reverts to normal size

Zooming the Display

If you want the items on the iPhone 8 screen to be larger, this can be done with the Display Zoom feature. To do this:

1 Tap once on the **Settings** app

2 Tap once on the **Display & Brightness** tab

3 Tap once on the **View** button underneath **Display Zoom**

4 Tap once on the **Standard** button to view the current settings. Tap once on the **Zoomed** button to see the increased size

The Display & Brightness settings can also be used to increase the text size for supported apps. Tap once on the **Text Size** button to access a slider with which you can set the required text size.

5 Tap once on the **Set** button to change the size of the items on the screen, then tap the **Zoomed** button to apply the change

Using 3D Touch

One of the features using touch on the iPhone 8 is 3D Touch. This can be used to activate different options for certain apps, depending on the strength with which you press on an item. For instance, a single press, or tap, can be used to open an app. However, if you press harder on the app then different options appear. This can be used for Quick Actions, and Peek and Pop.

Quick Actions

These are some of the Quick Actions that can be accessed with 3D Touch:

Hot tip

Accessing the 3D Touch features requires specific extra pressure: it is not just a case of pressing with the same amount of pressure for a longer time. This is known as pressing "deeper" into an app. This also provides a slight buzzing vibration, known as haptic feedback.

Don't forget

Most apps that have 3D Touch Quick Actions functionality are the pre-installed Apple ones. An increasing number of third-party apps also now support this; most notably social media apps such as Facebook and Twitter. Experiment by pressing deeper on different apps to see if they have options for 3D Touch.

1 Press deeper into the **Camera** app to access options for taking a selfie or recording a video, a slo-mo shot or a regular photo

2 Press deeper into the **Messages** app to access options for sending a text message to recent contacts or creating a new message

3 Press deeper into the **Mail** app to access options for adding a VIP, creating a new email, searching for an email, accessing your VIP email contacts or accessing your Inbox

Peek and Pop

3D Touch can also be used to view items within apps, with a single press. This is known as Peek and Pop. To use this, with the Mail app:

1 Press on an email in your Inbox to peek at it; i.e. view it with the other items blurred out

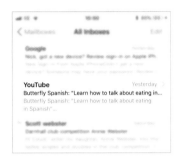

2 Press deeper on the email to pop it open; i.e. view it in Preview mode, rather than opening it fully. (Swipe up on the Preview screen to access a menu for options for the email, e.g. Reply etc.)

3 Press deeper again on the email to open it fully in the Mail app and access its full functionality

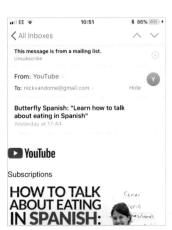

Don't forget

Other apps that offer Peek and Pop include: Safari, Maps, Camera and Photos. Items for Safari and Maps can be peeked at and accessed from within an email; e.g. if there is a website link in an email, press it once to view a preview of the web page and press deeper to open it in Safari. Photos can be peeked at from the Camera app by pressing on a thumbnail image and then pressing deeper to open it.

About Apple Pay

Apple Pay is Apple's service for mobile, contactless payment. It can be used by adding credit, debit and store cards to your iPhone 8, via the Wallet app, and then paying for items by using your Touch ID fingerprint as authorization for payment. Credit, debit and store cards have to be issued by banks or retailers who support Apple Pay, and there are an increasing number that do so, with more joining on a regular basis. Outlets also have to support Apple Pay but this, too, is increasing and, given the success of the iPhone, is likely to grow at a steady rate.

Setting up Apple Pay

To use Apple Pay you have to first add your cards to your iPhone 8 (and be signed in to iCloud):

Don't forget

At the time of printing, Apple Pay has no limit for in-store purchases in the US and, in the UK, the previous £30 limit has been lifted for most terminals. Visit **https://support. apple.com/en-us/ HT201469** for further information.

Hot tip

Cards can also be added to the Wallet at any time from **Settings** > **Wallet & Apple Pay** > **Add Credit or Debit Card**.

Don't forget

If your bank does not yet support Apple Pay then you will not be able to add your credit or debit card details into the Wallet app.

1 Tap once on the **Wallet** app

2 Tap once on the **Add Credit or Debit Card** link, or tap once on this button

Wallet

Pay with Touch ID using Apple Pay. Make purchases in stores and in apps without swiping your card or entering your card and shipping details.

Add Credit or Debit Card

3 Tap once on the **Continue** button

 Pay

Add credit, debit, or store cards and use Apple Pay with Touch ID to make purchases easily and securely, right from your iPhone.

Apple may use anonymous location data to improve its services. Your phone number, account, and location information may be sent to your card issuer to set up Apple Pay. About Apple Pay & Privacy...

Continue

...cont'd

4 The card details can be added to the Wallet by taking a photo of the card. Place the card on a flat surface, and position it within the white box. The card number is then added automatically. Alternatively, tap once on **Enter Card Details Manually**

Add Card

Position your card in the frame.

Enter Card Details Manually

Beware

Obtaining your card number using the camera is not always completely accurate. Take the photo in good light, always check the number afterwards, and amend it if necessary.

5 Once the card details have been added, your bank or store card issuer has to verify your card. This can be done either by a text message or a phone call

6 Once the Apple Pay wizard is completed, details of the card appear in the Wallet app

FROM SANTANDER

"Santander Debit Card" is ready for Apple Pay.

Don't forget

Although no form of contactless payment is 100% secure, Apple Pay does offer some security safeguards. One is that no card information is passed between the retailer and the user: the transaction is done by sending an encrypted token that is used to authorize the payment. Also, the use of the Touch ID fingerprint ensures another step of authorization that is not available with all other forms of contactless payment.

7 To pay for items with Apple Pay, open the **Wallet** app and tap once on the card you want to use. Hold your iPhone 8 up to the contactless payment card reader. Press the **Home** button to authorize the payment

Hold Near Reader to Pay

with Touch ID using your unique fingerprint. (Retailers must have a contactless card reader in order for Apple Pay to be used)

Beware

There is no separate headphone jack on the iPhone 8. Instead, headphones are connected via the Lightning connector jack. However, this means that earphones and headphones with a traditional jack will not work with the iPhone 8, unless the Lightning to 3.5mm headphone jack adapter is used (this is included with the iPhone 8 and 8 Plus).

Both models of the iPhone 8 can be used with the AirPods; the wireless headphones from Apple.

Using the EarPods

The iPhone EarPods are not only an excellent way to listen to music and other audio on your iPhone; they can also be used in a variety of ways with the phone function:

The EarPods contain three main controls:

Down volume   Up volume

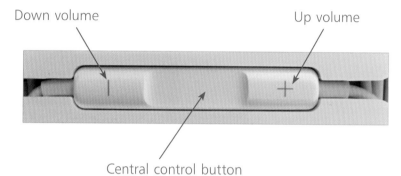

Central control button

- Plug in the EarPods to use them to hear someone who is calling you. Speak normally, and the other person will be able to hear you via the EarPods' in-built microphone.

- Click once in the middle of the control button to answer an incoming call.

- Press and hold in the middle of the control button for a couple of seconds (until you hear two beeps) to decline an incoming call.

- Click once in the middle of the control button to end the current call.

- If you are on a call and receive another one, click once on the middle of the control button to put the first call on hold and activate the second call.

- Press and hold the middle of the control button to dial a number using Voice Control, whereby you can speak the required number.

- Click on the control button when playing a music track to pause it. Click again to restart it. Double-click on the control button to move to the next track. Triple-click on the control button to move back to the previous track.

3 Head in the iCloud

iCloud, the online storage service, is at the heart of the iPhone for backing up your content and sharing it with other family members.

What is iCloud?

iCloud is the Apple online storage and backup service that performs a number of valuable functions:

It is free to register and set up a standard iCloud account.

Don't forget

An Apple ID can be created with an email address and password. It can then be used to access a variety of services, including the iTunes Store, iBooks and the App Store.

Hot tip

To access your iCloud account through the website, access www.icloud.com and enter your Apple ID details.

- It makes your content available across multiple devices. The content is stored in the iCloud and then pushed out to other iCloud-enabled devices, including the iPad, iPod Touch and other Mac or Windows computers.

- It enables online access to your content via the iCloud website. This includes your iCloud email, photos, contacts, calendar, reminders, and documents.

- It can back up the content on your iPhone.

To use iCloud you must have an Apple ID. This can be done when you first set up your iPhone, or at a later date. Once you have registered for and set up iCloud, it works automatically so you do not have to worry about anything.

1 Tap once on the **Settings** app

2 At the top of the Settings panel, tap once on the **Sign in to your iPhone** option

Settings

Q Search

Sign in to your iPhone
Set up iCloud, the App Store, and more.

3 If you already have an Apple ID, enter your details and tap once on the **Sign In** button

4 If you do not yet have an Apple ID, tap once on the **Don't have an Apple ID or forgot it?** link and follow the steps to create your Apple ID

Cancel   Sign In

Apple ID

Sign in with your Apple ID to use iCloud, iTunes, the App Store, and more.

Apple ID   nickvandome@mac.com

Password   ••••••••

Don't have an Apple ID or forgot it?

iCloud Settings

Once you have set up your iCloud account, you can then apply settings for how it works. Once you have done this, you will not have to worry about it again:

1 Tap once on the **Apple ID** section in the Settings app

2 Tap once on the **iCloud** button

3 Drag these buttons to **On** for each item that you wish to be included in iCloud. Each item is then saved and stored in the iCloud and made available to your other iCloud-enabled devices

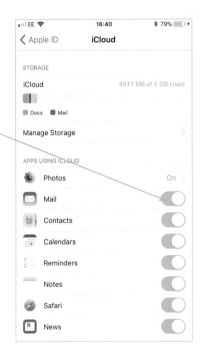

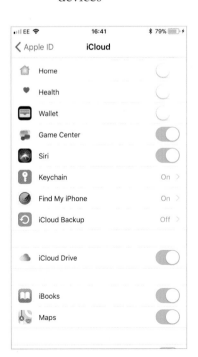

Adding iCloud Storage

By default, you get 5GB of free storage space with an iCloud account. However, you can upgrade this if you want to increase the amount of storage. To do this:

1 Access **iCloud** in Settings, as shown on page 53

2 Tap once on the **Manage Storage** button to view how your iCloud storage is being used

3 Tap once on the **Upgrade** button if you want to increase the amount of iCloud storage

4 Tap once on one of the storage options to buy this amount of iCloud storage (Note: charges appear in your local currency)

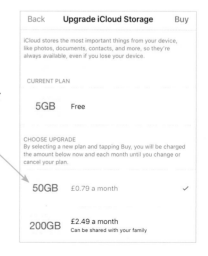

Backing up with iCloud

All of the items that you have assigned to iCloud
(see page 53) should be backed up there automatically.
However, if this is not happening you may need to turn on
the iCloud Backup. To do this:

1 Within the
iCloud section
of the Settings app,
tap once on the **iCloud Backup** button, if it is Off

2 The iCloud
Backup button
will be **Off**

(see page 53)

3 Drag the **iCloud Backup** button to **On** to enable
automatic backup for iCloud. This has to be done
over Wi-Fi, with the iPhone locked and plugged in

4 You can also back up manually at any time by
tapping once on the **Back Up Now** button

Hot tip

You can also back
up your iPhone to
a computer that
has iTunes. Connect
the iPhone to the
computer with the
Lightning/USB cable,
and open iTunes.
Click on
this button
on the top
toolbar and, under
the **Summary** tab,
click on the **Back Up
Now** button under
the **Manually Back
up and Restore**
heading.

About Family Sharing

As everyone gets more and more digital devices, it is becoming increasingly important to be able to share content with other people, particularly family members. In iOS 11, the Family Sharing function enables you to share items that you have downloaded from the App Store, such as music and movies, with up to six other family members, as long as they have an Apple ID Account. Once this has been set up, it is also possible to share items such as family calendars and photos, and even see where family members are on a map. To set up and start using Family Sharing:

Beware

To use Family Sharing, the other members of the group need to have iOS 8 (or later) installed on their mobile devices, or OS X Yosemite (or later) on an Apple desktop or laptop computer.

1 Access the Apple ID section within the Settings app, as shown on page 53

2 Tap once on the **Set Up Family Sharing...** link

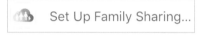

Set Up Family Sharing...

3 Tap once on the **Get Started** button

Cancel

Family Sharing

Share music, movies, apps, storage and more with up to six members of your family.

You'll also get a family photo album, family calendar, and access to family devices in Find My iPhone.

Get Started

Learn more about Family Sharing

4 Tap once on the first item you want to share via Family Sharing. This includes music, iCloud storage plans, iTunes and App Store purchases, and location sharing for finding a lost or stolen Apple device

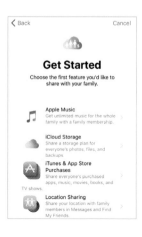

‹ Back   Cancel

Get Started

Choose the first feature you'd like to share with your family.

Apple Music
Get unlimited music for the whole family with a family membership.

iCloud Storage
Share a storage plan for everyone's photos, files, and backups.

iTunes & App Store Purchases
Share everyone's purchased apps, music, movies, books, and TV shows.

Location Sharing
Share your location with family members in Messages and Find My Friends.

5 Tap once on the **Continue** button again to confirm your Apple ID account for Family Sharing

6 If you are the organizer of Family Sharing, payments will be taken from the credit/debit card that you registered when you set up your Apple ID. Tap once on the **Continue** button to confirm this

7 Once Family Sharing has been created, return to the iCloud section in the Settings app and tap once on the **Invite Via iMessage** button

When you invite someone to Family Sharing you can specify that they have to ask permission before downloading content from the iTunes Store, the App Store or the iBooks Store. To do this, select the family member in the **Family** section of the **iCloud** settings, and drag the **Ask To Buy** button to **On**. Each time they want to buy something you will be sent a notification asking for approval. This is a good option if grandchildren are added to the Family Sharing group.

8 Enter the name or email address of a family member, and tap once on the **Send** button

9 An invitation is sent to the selected person. They have to accept this before they can participate in Family Sharing

Using Family Sharing

Once you have set up Family Sharing and added family members, you can start sharing a selection of items.

Sharing photos

Photos can be shared with Family Sharing, thanks to the Family album that is created automatically within the Photos app. To use this:

Beware

iCloud Photo Sharing has to be turned **On** to enable Family Sharing for photos (**Settings** > **Photos** > **iCloud Photo Sharing**).

Hot tip

When someone else in your Family Sharing circle adds a photo to the Family album, you are notified in the Notification Center and also by a red notification on the Photos app.

1. Tap once on the **Photos** app

2. Tap once on the **Shared** button

3. The **Family** album is already available in the **Shared** section. Tap once on the blank album, and start adding photos to it

Family
From You

4. Tap once on this button to add photos to the album

5. Tap once on the photos you want to add, and tap once on the **Done** button

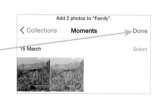

6. Make sure the **Family** album is selected as the Shared Album, and tap once on the **Post** button

Sharing calendars

Family Sharing also generates a Family calendar that can be used by all Family Sharing members:

1 Tap once on the **Calendar** app

2 Tap once on this button to create a New Event. The current calendar will probably not be the Family one. Tap once on the calendar name to change it

3 Tap once on the **Family** calendar

4 The **Family** calendar is now selected for the event

Calendar ● Family >

5 Complete the details for the event. It will be added to your calendar, with the **Family** tag. Other people in your Family Sharing circle will have this  event added to their Family calendar too, and they will be sent a notification

Don't forget

When someone in the Family Sharing circle adds an event to the Family calendar it will appear in your calendar with the appropriate tag. A red notification will also appear on the Calendar app, and it will appear in the Notification Center (if the Calendar has been selected to appear here).

Don't forget

Tap once on the **Add** button to invite other people by email (they do not have to be part of Family Sharing, but they do have to accept your invitation to be part of Find My Friends).

Don't forget

Tap once on your own name at the bottom-left of the screen to see your settings for Find My Friends. This is where you can share your location. Share My Location also has to be turned on within **Settings** > **Privacy** > **Location Services** > **Share My Location**.

...cont'd

Finding family members

Family Sharing makes it easy to keep in touch with the rest of the family and see exactly where they are. This can be done with the Find Friends app. The other person must have their iPhone (or other Apple device) turned on, be online and be sharing their location. To do this:

1 Tap once on the **Find Friends** app

2 Your own location has to be shared if you want other people to see it. Tap once on the **Me** button at the bottom of the window, and drag the **Share My Location** button to On

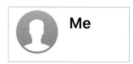

3 The details of any people who are linked via your Family Sharing are displayed. Tap once on a person's name to view their details and location in the top panel (if they are online and have shared their location on their device)

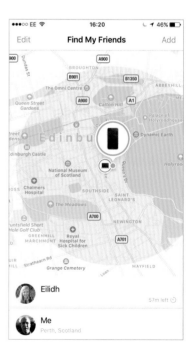

Sharing apps, music, books and movies

Family Sharing means that all members of the group can share purchases from the iTunes Store, the App Store or the iBooks store. To do this:

1 Open either **App Store, iTunes Store** or **iBooks**

2 For the **App Store**, tap once on the Account icon and tap once on the **Purchased** button;

or,

for the **iTunes Store**, tap once on the **More** button on the bottom toolbar and tap once on the **Purchased** button;

or, for **iBooks**, tap once on the **Purchased** button on the bottom toolbar

3 For all three apps, tap once on a member under **Family Purchases** to view their purchases and download them, if required, by tapping once on this button

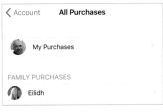

Don't forget

Using Family Sharing, other members of the group will be able to access and download the content that you have purchased, too.

iCloud Drive and the Files App

The Files app is a new feature in iOS 11 on the iPhone.

One of the features of iCloud is the iCloud Drive, which can be used to store documents such as those created with the Apple suite of productivity apps (available in the App Store): Pages, (word processing), Numbers (spreadsheets) and Keynote (presentations). These documents can then be accessed with the Files app.

The Files app can also be used with other online storage services, such as Dropbox and Google Drive, if you have one of these accounts. If so, they will appear under the **Locations** section in Step 3.

1 Access the **iCloud** settings as shown on page 53, and drag the **iCloud Drive** button to **On**. Drag **On** the buttons for any compatible apps that you want to use with iCloud Drive

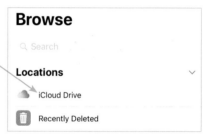
iCloud Drive

2 Tap once on the **Files** app

Files

3 Tap once on the **iCloud Drive** button to view its contents

Browse

Q Search

Locations

iCloud Drive

Recently Deleted

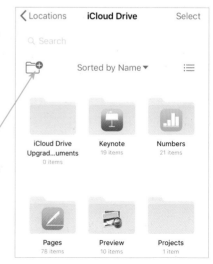

Tap once on the **Select** button at the top of any folder, and tap once on an item to select it. Then use these buttons to, from left to right, share the selected item, duplicate an item, move an item, or delete an item.

4 Tap once on individual folders to view their contents (this will include documents created in their respective apps). Tap once on this button to add folders, either to the top level, or within specific sub-folders in the Files app

Locations · iCloud Drive · Select

Q Search

Sorted by Name ▾

iCloud Drive Upgrad...uments · 0 items

Keynote · 19 items

Numbers · 21 items

Pages · 78 items

Preview · 10 items

Projects · 1 item

4 Calls and Contacts

One of the main uses for the iPhone is still to make and receive phone calls. This chapter shows what you need for this.

Adding Contacts

Because of its power and versatility, it is sometimes forgotten that one of the reasons for the iPhone's existence is to make phone calls. Before you start doing this, it is a good idea to add family and friends to the Contacts app. This will enable you to phone them without having to tap in their phone number each time. To add a contact:

1 Tap once on the **Contacts** app

2 Any contacts that you already have are displayed

3 Tap once on this button to add a new contact

Tap once on the green button next to a field to add another field. Tap once on a red button to delete a field.

4 Enter the name for the contact at the top of the window, in the **First name** and **Last name** fields

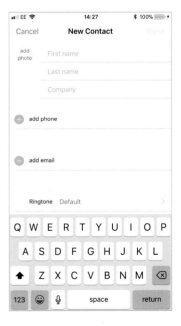

5 Tap once in one of the Phone fields, or tap once on the **add phone** button to add a new Phone field

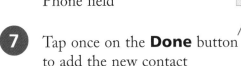

6 Enter the required number with the number pad that is activated when you tap in a Phone field

7 Tap once on the **Done** button to add the new contact

Done

8 The contact is added under **Contacts**

Groups	Contacts	+
Q Search		
V		
Lucy **Vandome**		
Mark **Vandome**		A

9 Tap once on a contact to view their full details. You can use these buttons at the top of the window to send them a text; make a voice call to them; make a video, or voice, call using FaceTime; or send them an email (if their email address is included)

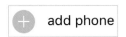

Lucy Vandome

message   call   FaceTime   home

home
07

mobile

FaceTime

home
lucy@

Hot tip

Use the buttons at the bottom of a contact's window to send them a message, share their details with other people, add them as a favorite or share your location with them. If someone is added as a favorite, they can be accessed directly from the **Favorites** button on the bottom toolbar of the **Phone** app.

Favorites   Recents   Contacts

Making a Call

The iPhone 8 can be used to make calls to specific phone numbers that you enter manually, or to contacts in your Contacts app.

Dialing a number

To make a call by dialing a specific number, first tap once on the **Phone** app.

1 Tap once on the **Keypad** button at the bottom of the window

Keypad

2 Tap on the numbers on the keypad to enter the number, which appears at the top of the window. Tap on this button to delete a number that has been entered

3 Tap once on this button to make the call

66

Calling a contact

To call someone who has been added to the Contacts app:

1 Open the **Phone** app, and tap once on the **Contacts** button at the bottom of the window. The Contacts app opens, with the Phone toolbar still visible at the bottom of the window

Contacts

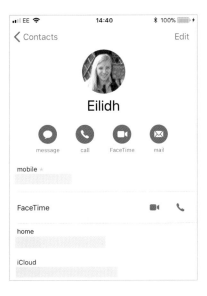

2 Tap once on a contact

3 The full details for the contact are displayed. Tap once on the **call** button at the top of the window to call the number of the contact

call

Hot tip

To find someone in the Contacts app (either directly from the app, or from the **Contacts** button in the Phone app), swipe up and down on the screen; enter a name in the Search box at the top of the window; or tap on a letter on the alphabetic list down the right-hand side.

67

Receiving a Call

When you receive a call, there are four main options:

Don't forget

When a call is connected, the following buttons appear on the screen. Use them to: mute a call; access the keypad again, in case you need to add any more information, such as for an automated call; access the speaker so you do not have to keep the phone at your ear; add another call to create a conference call; make a FaceTime call to the caller (if they have this facility); or access your Contacts app.

1 When you receive a call, the person's name and photo (if they have been added to your Contacts), or number, appears at the top of the screen

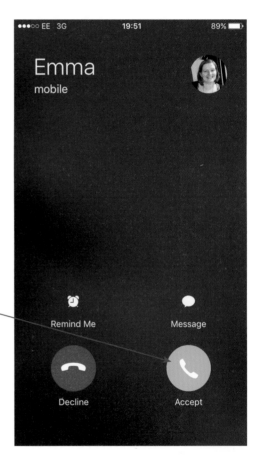

2 Tap once on the **Accept** button (or if the phone is locked, drag the **slide to answer** button to the right) to take the call

3 Tap once on the **Decline** button to decline the call, without any other actions. If the phone is locked when a call comes in, press the phone's **On/Off** button to decline the call. This is then displayed at the top of the window:

4 Tap once on the **Remind Me** button to decline the call but set a reminder for yourself that the person has called

5 Select an option for when you want to be reminded

The reminder in Step 5 will appear on the Lock screen and also as a notification in the Notification Center (if this has been specified).

6 Tap once on the **Message** button to decline the call but send the person a text message instead

7 Tap once on the text message that you want to send

Tap once on this button to end a call.

Saving Phone Contacts

Another quick way to add a contact is to ask someone to phone you so that you can then copy their number directly from your phone to your Contacts. You do not even have to answer the phone to do this.

1 Once someone has phoned, tap once on the **Phone** app

2 Tap once on the **Recents** button at the bottom of the window

Recents

3 The call will be displayed. Tap once on the **i** symbol

| All | Missed | Edit |

07
United Kingdom
8/9/17 (i)

4 Information about the call is displayed, including the number

Hot tip

Information from a caller can also be added to an existing contact. For instance, if one of your contacts calls you from a different phone, these details can be added to their existing information. To do this, tap once on the **Add to Existing Contact** button in Step 5.

5 Tap once on the **Create New Contact** button

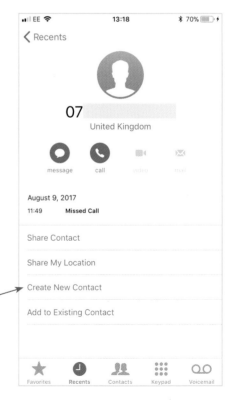

6 The New Contact window opens, with the number already pre-inserted

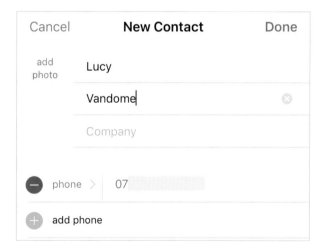

7 Add information for the contact, as required, such as name, any additional phone numbers, and email

8 Tap once on the **Done** button to add the new contact

Setting Ringtones

Ringtones were one of the original "killer apps" for mobile/cell phones: the must-have accessory that helped transform the way people looked at these devices. The iPhone has a range of ringtones that can be used, and you can also download and install thousands more. To use the default ringtones:

72

1 Tap once on the **Settings** app

Settings

2 Tap once on the **Sounds** tab

Sounds

3 Tap once on the **Ringtone** link under **Sounds and Vibration Patterns** to select ringtones for when you receive a phone call

SOUNDS AND VIBRATION PATTERNS

Ringtone   Opening >

4 Tap once on one of the options to hear a preview and select it

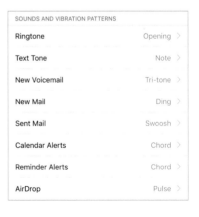
RINGTONES

✓ Opening (Default)

Apex

Beacon

Bulletin

5 Sounds and vibrations can also be selected for a range of other items, such as email, FaceTime calls, Facebook posts and calendar and reminder alerts, by going back to the Sounds and Vibration Patterns section and choosing a tone for each item

SOUNDS AND VIBRATION PATTERNS

Ringtone   Opening >

Text Tone   Note >

New Voicemail   Tri-tone >

New Mail   Ding >

Sent Mail   Swoosh >

Calendar Alerts   Chord >

Reminder Alerts   Chord >

AirDrop   Pulse >

Adding individual ringtones

It is also possible to set ringtones for individual people, so that you know immediately who a call is from.

1 Select a contact in the Contacts app, and tap on the **Edit** button

Beware

Only set ringtones for your most regular contacts, otherwise you may end up with too many variations.

2 Tap once on the **Ringtone** button

3 Tap once on a ringtone to assign this to the contact

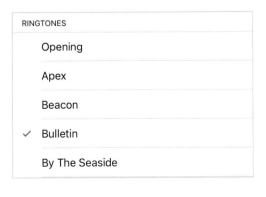

Beware

If you are going to be using your iPhone around other people, consider turning the **Keyboard Clicks** option (at the bottom of the main Sounds window) to **Off**, as the noise can get annoying for those in the vicinity.

Phone Settings

As with most of the iPhone functions, there is a range of settings for the phone itself. To use them:

1 Tap once on the **Settings** app

2 Tap once on the **Phone** tab

3 The Phone settings have options for responding with a text to a call that you do not take; call forwarding; call waiting; and blocking unwanted callers

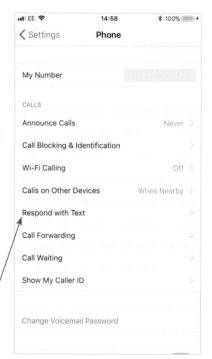

4 Tap once on the **Respond with Text** button to create a text message that can be sent if you do not want to answer a call when it is made

5 Typing and Texts

This chapter shows how to get used to the virtual keyboard for adding text, and how to use the texting options, including the range of items that can be added to messages with iOS 11, such as stickers and photos.

The iPhone Keyboard

The keyboard on the iPhone is a virtual one; i.e. it appears on the touchscreen whenever text or numbered input is required for an app. This can be for a variety of reasons:

- Entering text with a word processing app, or into an email or an organizing app such as Notes.

- Entering a web address in a web browser such as the Safari app.

- Entering information into an online form.

- Entering a password.

Viewing the keyboard

When you attempt one of the actions above, the keyboard appears so that you can enter any text or numbers:

Shift button

Space bar

Around the keyboard

To access the various keyboard controls:

1. Tap once on the **Shift** button to create a **Cap** (capital) text letter

2. Double-tap on the **Shift** button to enable **Caps Lock**

3. Tap once on this button to back-delete an item

Hot tip

In some apps, such as Notes, Mail and Messages, it is possible to change the keyboard into a trackpad for moving the cursor. To do this, press and hold firmly on the keyboard, and then swipe over the trackpad to move the cursor around.

Hot tip

It is possible to increase the size of the iPhone keyboard with the **Zoom** feature within the Accessibility settings. See pages 180-181 for details.

Don't forget

To return from Caps Lock, tap once on the **Caps** button.

4 Tap once on this button to access the **Numbers** keyboard option

5 From the Numbers keyboard, tap once on this button to access the **Symbols** keyboard

6 Tap once on this button on either of the two keyboards above to return to the standard QWERTY option

ABC

Shortcut keys

Instead of having to go to a different keyboard every time you want to add punctuation (or numbers), there is a shortcut for this:

1 Press and hold on the **Numbers** button, and swipe over the item you want to include. This will be added, and you will remain on the QWERTY keyboard

Keyboard Settings

Settings for the keyboard can be determined in the General section of the Settings app. To do this:

Hot tip

Drag the **Predictive** button to **On** to enable predictive texting (see pages 80-81). Drag the **Character Preview** button to **On** to show a magnified example of a letter or symbol when it is pressed, to ensure that the correct one is selected.

Hot tip

The Auto-Correction function works as you type a word, so it may change a number of times, depending on the length of the word you are typing.

1 Tap once on the **Settings** app

2 Tap once on the **General** tab

3 Tap once on the **Keyboard** link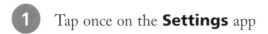

4 Drag the **Auto-Capitalization** button to **On** to automatically capitalize letters at the beginning of a sentence

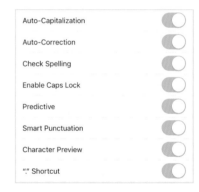

5 Drag the **Auto-Correction** button to **On** to enable suggestions for words to appear as you type, particularly if you have mistyped a word

6 Drag the **Check Spelling** and **Smart Punctuation** buttons to **On** to identify misspelled words (with red underlining) and add punctuation

7 Drag the **Enable Caps Lock** button to **On** to enable this function to be performed

8 Drag the **"." Shortcut** button to **On** to add a period (full stop) and a space to start a new sentence by just tapping the space bar twice

9 Tap once on the **Text Replacement** link to view existing text shortcuts and also to create new ones

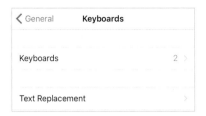

10 Tap once on this button to create new shortcuts

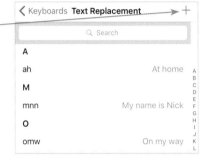

Hot tip

With iOS 11, third-party keyboards can be downloaded from the App Store and used instead of the default one. Two to look at are SwiftKey Keyboard and Swype.

11 Enter a phrase and the shortcut you want to use to create it when you type. Tap once on the **Save** button

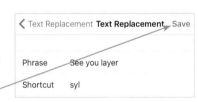

Don't forget

By default, two keyboards are installed: one for the language of your region, and the emoji one. If more keyboards are added, this symbol will appear

12 Tap once on the **Keyboards** button in Step 9 to add a new keyboard

13 Tap once on the **Add New Keyboard...** button

Add New Keyboard...

14 Tap once on a keyboard to add it. The keyboard will be available by selecting the globe icon (see the Don't Forget tip)

on the keyboard. Press on it to select another keyboard from the one being used. If only the two default keyboards are installed, this symbol will be the emoji one.

Using Predictive Text

Predictive text tries to guess what you are typing, and also predicts the next word following the one you have just typed. It is excellent for text messaging.

To use it:

1 Tap once on the **General** tab in the Settings app

2 Tap once on the **Keyboard** link

3 Drag the **Predictive** button **On**

4 When predictive text is activated, the QuickType bar is displayed above the keyboard. Initially, this has a suggestion for the first word to include. Tap on a word, or start typing

5 As you type, suggestions appear. Tap on one to accept it. Tap on the word within the quotation marks to accept exactly what you have typed

Don't forget

Predictive text learns from your writing style as you write, and so gets more accurate at predicting words. It can also recognize a change in style for different apps, such as Mail and Messages.

6 If you continue typing, the predictive suggestions will change as you add more letters

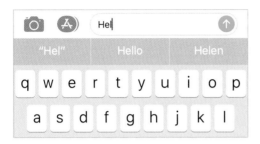

7 After you have typed a word, a suggestion for the next word appears. Tap on one of the suggestions, or start typing a new word, which will then also have predictive suggestions as you type

Toggling predictive text from the keyboard
You can also toggle predictive text On or Off from the keyboard. To do this:

1 Press and hold on this button on the keyboard

2 Tap once on the **Keyboard Settings...** button to access the **Predictive** setting, from where it can be turned **On** or **Off**

Keyboard Settings...

English (US)

Emoji

123   space

Hot tip

Tapping the button in Step 1 allows you to add Emojis, which are symbols used in text messages to signify happiness, surprise, sadness, etc. (See page 90 for details.)

One Handed Keyboard

When typing with the iPhone, this is frequently done with one hand. To make this easier, there is an option for formatting the keyboard for one handed typing. To do this:

One handed typing is a new feature on the iPhone with iOS 11.

1 Open the **General** tab in the Settings app, and tap once on the **One Handed Keyboard** link

‹ General	**Keyboards**	
Keyboards		2 ›
Text Replacement		›
One Handed Keyboard		Off ›

2 Select the **Left** or **Right** option for the keyboard

‹ Back	**One Handed Keyboard**	
Off		
Left		✓
Right		

3 If more than one keyboard has been added, e.g. the emoji keyboard, press and hold on this button on the keyboard, and tap once on the options for moving the keyboard to the left or right

4 The keyboard is moved into the position selected in either Steps 2 or 3. Tap once here to revert to the original keyboard

Entering Text

Once you have applied the keyboard settings that you require, you can start entering text. To do this:

1 Tap once on the screen to activate the keyboard from the app. Start typing with the keyboard. The text will appear at the point where you tapped on the screen

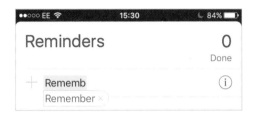

2 As you type, Auto-Correction comes up with suggestions (if it is turned on). Tap once on the space bar to accept the suggestion, or tap once on the cross next to it to reject it

3 If Check Spelling is enabled in the keyboard settings, any misspelled words appear underlined in red

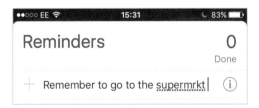

4 Double-tap the space bar to enter a period (full-stop) and a space at the end of a sentence

If you keep typing as normal, the Auto-Correction suggestion will disappear when you finish the word.

If Predictive text is turned **On** (**Settings** > **General** > **Keyboard** > **Predictive**) the Auto-Correction suggestions will appear on the QuickType bar above the keyboard.

The **"."Shortcut** option has to be turned **On** (**Settings** > **General** > **Keyboard** > **"." Shortcut**) for the functionality in Step 4 to work (see page 78).

Editing Text

Once text has been entered it can be selected, copied, cut and pasted. Depending on the app being used, the text can also be formatted, such as with a word processing app.

Selecting text
To select text and perform tasks on it:

Hot tip

Once the selection buttons have been accessed, tap once on **Select** to select the previous word, or **Select All** to select all of the text.

Hot tip

In some apps, such as Notes, Mail and Messages, it is possible to change the keyboard into a trackpad for moving the cursor. To do this, press and hold firmly on the keyboard, and then swipe over the trackpad to move the cursor around.

1 To change the insertion point, tap and hold until the magnifying glass appears

2 Drag the magnifying glass to move the insertion point

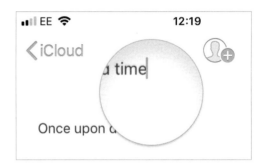

3 Tap once at the insertion point to access the selection buttons

4 Double-tap on a word to select it. Tap once on **Cut** or **Copy**, as required

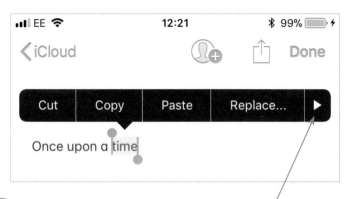

5 Tap once here to view additional options

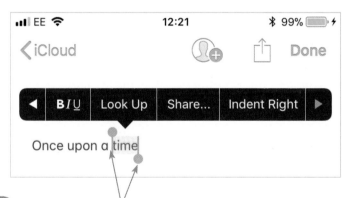

6 Drag the selection handles to expand or contract the selection

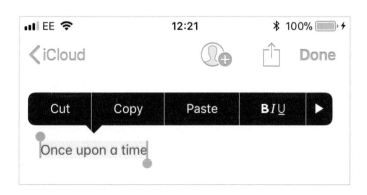

Hot tip

The selection buttons in Steps 4 and 5 can also be used to replace the selected word; add bold, italics or underlining to it; view a definition (Look Up) of it; share it; or indent it. (These options may change depending on the app you're in, and whether the iPhone is held in portrait or landscape mode.)

Types of Text Messages

Text messaging should not be thought of as the domain of the younger generation. On your iPhone, you can join the world of text with the Apple iMessage service that is accessed via the Messages app. This enables text, photo, video and audio messages to be sent, free of charge, between users of iOS on the iPhone, iPad, iPod Touch, and Mac computers with OS X or macOS.

However, there are two different types of text messages:

- iMessages that are sent over Wi-Fi, to other users with an Apple ID and using an iPhone, iPad, iPod Touch or a Mac computer.

- Text messages that are just sent via your cellular (mobile) carrier.

Wi-Fi texts (iMessages)

When texts are sent over Wi-Fi, this can only be done with other users who have an Apple ID.

When you are connected to Wi-Fi, this symbol appears at the top of your iPhone.

To use iMessages over Wi-Fi, the **iMessage** button has to be **On**, in the **Messages** section of the Settings app.

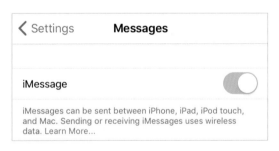

Cellular (mobile) carrier texts (SMS)

When texts are sent via your mobile carrier, this can be done to any cellular (mobile) number.

When you are connected to your cellular (mobile) carrier this symbol appears at the top of your iPhone, with the appropriate carrier's name.

Sending an iMessage via Wi-Fi

When you send an iMessage, it appears in a blue bubble.

If you enter a number that is not connected to an Apple ID account then the message will be sent as an SMS (green bubble) rather than an iMessage (blue bubble).

Sending a text via your carrier

When you send a text via your cellular (mobile) carrier, it appears in a green bubble.

iMessages can also be used to send money to other people. This is done using Apple Pay, and the recipient also has to have Apple Pay, enabled. The sum of money is entered into an iMessage to the recipient and then sent by using Touch ID. The money is kept as Apple Pay Cash within the recipient's Wallet app and can be used to pay for items using Apple Pay in stores or on the web, where this is available. This is a new feature in iOS 11 on the iPhone.

87

Text Messaging

The process for sending text messages is the same for either iMessages or SMS text messages:

1 Tap once on the **Messages** app

2 You have to sign in with your Apple ID before you can use Messages. Enter these details, and tap on the **Sign In** button

3 Tap once on this button to create a new message and start a new conversation

4 Tap once on this button to select someone from your contacts

5 Tap once on a contact to select them as the recipient of the new message

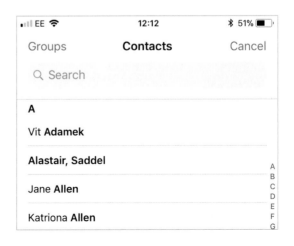

Don't forget

You can also enter a cell/mobile phone number into the **To:** field for text messages in Messages. If this is connected to an Apple ID, the message will be sent as an iMessage; if not, it will be sent as an SMS message.

Hot tip

You can also add someone from your contacts by typing their name into the **To:** field shown in Step 4. As you start typing, names will appear for you to select from. You can type the telephone number of anyone who isn't in your contacts here, too.

6 Tap once here, and type with the keyboard to create a message

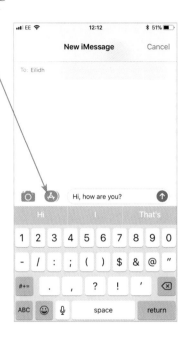

Don't forget

When a message has been sent, you are notified underneath it when it has been delivered.

7 Tap once on this button to send a message (it is not available until a message has been composed)

8 As the conversation progresses, each message is displayed in the main window

Hot tip

Press and hold on a message, and tap on the **More...** button that appears. Select a message, or messages, and tap on the **Trash** icon to remove them from the threads. (See pages 97-98 for more information on deleting messages.)

Enhancing Text Messages

Adding emojis

Emojis (small graphical symbols) are becoming more common in text messages, and there is now a huge range that can be included with iOS 11. To add these:

1 Tap once on this button on the keyboard to view the emoji keyboards

2 Swipe left and right to view the emoji options. Tap once on an emoji to add it to a message

Emojis can be added automatically from certain words:

1 Add text, and tap once on the button in Step 1 above. The items that can be replaced are highlighted

| > | I like to eat cake on a train | ↑ |

| > | I like to eat cake on a train | ↑ |

2 Tap once on a highlighted word to see the emoji options. Tap once on one to add it to the message

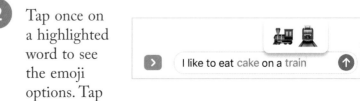

| > | I like to eat cake on a train | ↑ |

90

Full-screen messages
iMessages can also be sent with full-screen effects:

1 Write a message, and press and hold on this button

2 Tap once on the **Screen** button at the top of the window

3 Different animated options can be selected to accompany the message

4 Swipe to the left, or tap on these buttons to view different animated effects

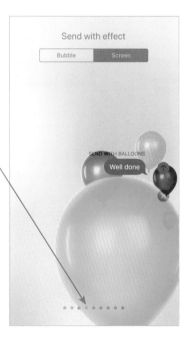

5 Tap once on this button to send the message (tap once on the cross to delete the animated effect)

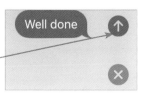

With Messages you can show people your location (by sending a map) rather than just telling them. To do this: Once a conversation has started, tap once on the **i** button at the top of the message window. Tap once on the **Send My Current Location**, or **Share My Location** buttons.

Send My Current Location

Share My Location

For **Share My Location**, options can be selected for **Share for One Hour**, **Share Until End of Day** or **Share Indefinitely**. If you select **Share My Location**, this will be updated if your location changes (as long as Location Services is turned On in **Settings** > **Privacy** > **Location Services**).

...cont'd

Invisible messages

There are several ways to enhance text messages, including sending them in a digital version of invisible ink:

Hot tip

While creating a message, tap once here for the options for adding different types of content, including adding stickers, digital touch items and photos (see pages 94-95).

Hot tip

The other Bubble effects in Step 2 are **Slam**, **Loud** and **Gentle**. These determine how the speech bubble appears to the recipient: Slam moves in quickly from left to right; Loud appears initially as a large bubble; Gentle appears initially with small text in the speech bubble. After the initial effects, the bubble returns to its normal size.

1 Write a message and press on this button

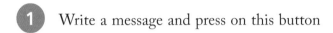

2 Tap once on the **Bubble** button at the top of the window

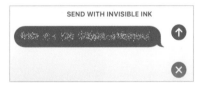

3 Tap once on the **Invisible Ink** button

4 Tap once on this button to send the invisible message

SEND WITH INVISIBLE INK

5 The message is sent as a bubble where the content is obscured

6 Swipe on the message to view its content

This is a top secret message!

Handwritten messages

To create a more informal message, handwriting can be used.

1 Turn the iPhone into landscape mode, and tap once on this button on the keyboard to access the handwriting panel

2 Write using your finger, or select one of the pre-formatted messages at the bottom of the

panel. Tap once on the **Done** button to add it to a message. The text appears animated to the recipient, as if it is being written on their screen

Quick replies (Tapback)

Instead of writing a full reply to a message it is possible to add a quick reply (also known as Tapback), which consists of an appropriate icon that is attached to the original message:

1 Press and hold on the message to which you want to add a quick reply, and tap once on one of the icons

2 The selected icon is added to the original message, and this is displayed to the sender of the message

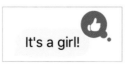

Hot tip

You can also send family and friends audio clips in an iMessage so that they can hear from you too. To do this, press and hold on the microphone icon at the right-hand side of the text field, and record your message.

The app drawer has been redesigned in iOS 11 on the iPhone.

If the button in Step 1 is not showing, i.e. if you are writing a message, tap once on this button to the left of the text field box.

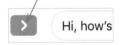

Music from your iTunes Library can also be added to an iMessage, from this button in Step 4.

...cont'd

Adding apps and stickers from the app drawer

Stickers and graphics are another option for enhancing text messages. To do this:

1 Tap once on this button to the left of the text field box to access the app drawer

2 Tap once on this button on the bottom toolbar

3 Tap once on the **Visit Store** button to view sticker sets and apps that can be included in messages

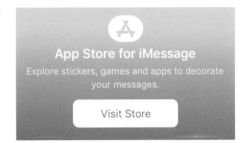

4 Navigate the content in the App Store to find apps to download as required, e.g. a set of stickers

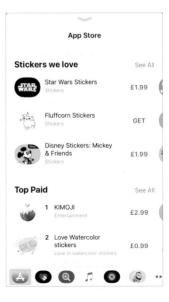

5 Downloaded items will be available in the app drawer. Tap once on one to view its available content

6 For stickers, tap once on a sticker to add it to a message

Don't forget

Tap once on the cross next to a sticker or an image to delete it, after it has been added to a message.

7 Tap once on this button in the app drawer to access animated images that can be added to messages in the same way as for stickers

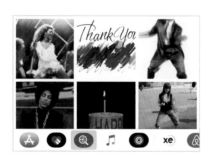

Adding photos and videos

To add photos or videos to a message:

1 Tap once on this button to the left of the message text field to add a photo or video, either by taking it from the iPhone's **Camera** app or by selecting one from your **Photo Library**

Hot tip

Tap once on this button in the app drawer to add Digital Touch effects. These are colorful animated effects that can be drawn on the screen and sent in a message.

Voice Typing

On the keyboard there is also a voice typing option, which enables you to enter text by speaking into a microphone, rather than typing on the keyboard. This is On by default.

Using voice typing

Voice typing (dictation) can be used with any app with a text input function. To do this:

Beware

Voice typing is not an exact science, and you may find that some strange examples appear. The best results are created if you speak as clearly as possible and reasonably slowly.

Hot tip

Dictation can be turned **On** or **Off** in **Settings** > **General** > **Keyboard** > **Enable Dictation**.

1 Tap once on this button on the keyboard to activate the voice typing microphone. Speak into the microphone to record text

2 As the voice typing function is processing the recording, this screen appears

3 Tap once on the **Keyboard** button to finish recording and return to the standard keyboard

4 Once the recording has been processed, the text appears in the app

Don't forget

There are other voice typing apps available from the App Store. One to try is Dragon Anywhere.

Managing Messages

Text conversations with individuals can become quite lengthy so it is sometimes a good idea to remove some messages, while still keeping the conversation going.

1 As a conversation with one person progresses, it moves downwards in the window

2 Press and hold on a message that you want to delete, and tap once on the **More...** button (pressing and holding on a message also activates the Tapback option; see page 93)

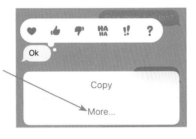

3 Tap once next to any message that you want to delete, so that a white tick in a blue circle appears

4 Tap once on the Trash icon to delete the selected message(s)

Hot tip

You can copy a message by tapping once on the **Copy** button in Step 2 and then pasting it into another app, such as an email. To do this, press and hold on an open email, and tap once on the **Paste** button.

Hot tip

Settings for the Messages app can be applied in the Settings app. These include: Send Read Receipts, to indicate that you have read the message sent; and to send SMS messages when iMessage is unavailable.

...cont'd

Whole conversations can also be deleted:

1 From a conversation, tap once on the **Back** button to view all of your conversations

2 Tap once on the **Edit** button

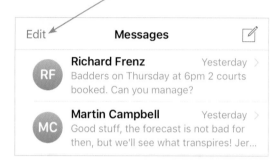

It is good housekeeping to delete conversations that have finished, otherwise you may end up with a long list of different ones.

3 Tap once next to any whole conversation(s) that you want to delete

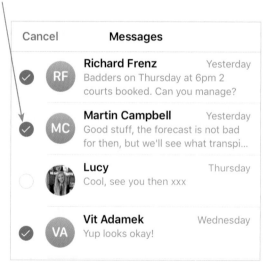

4 Tap once on the **Delete** button at the bottom right-hand corner of the screen to remove the selected conversation(s)

6 The Online World

This chapter shows how to use your iPhone to keep ahead in the fast-moving world of online communications, using the web, email, social media and video calls.

Getting Online

Connecting to Wi-Fi is one of the main ways that the iPhone can get online access. You will need to have an Internet Service Provider and a Wi-Fi router to connect to the internet. Once this is in place, you will be able to connect to a Wi-Fi network:

1 Tap once on the **Settings** app

2 Tap once on the **Wi-Fi** tab

3 Ensure the **Wi-Fi** button is in the **On** position

4 Available networks are shown here. Tap once on one to select it

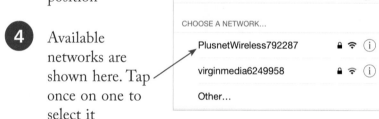

5 Enter a password for your Wi-Fi router

6 Tap once on the **Join** button Join

7 Once a network has been joined, a tick appears next to it. This now provides access to the internet

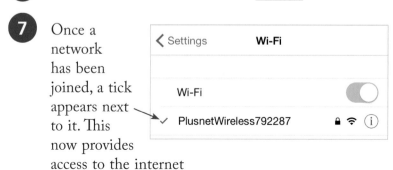

Safari Settings

Safari is the default web browser on the iPhone 8, and it can be used to bring the web to your iPhone. Before you start using Safari, there is a range of settings that can be applied:

1 Tap once on the **Settings** app

2 Tap once on the **Safari** tab

3 Make selections under the **Search** section for the default search engine, options for suggestions appearing as you type search words and phrases, and preloading the top-rating page in a search

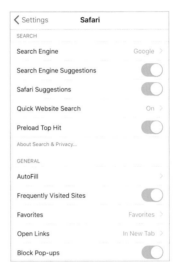

4 Make selections under the **General** section for entering passwords, specifying the items for the Favorites window, and blocking pop-ups

5 Make selections under the **Privacy & Security** section for blocking cookies, warning about fraudulent websites, checking to see whether websites accept Apple Pay, and clearing your web browsing history and web data

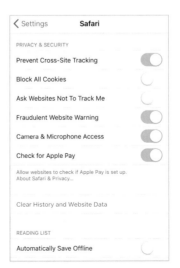

Because of the proliferation of apps available for the iPhone, you may find that you use Safari less than on a desktop or laptop computer. For example, most major news outlets have their own apps that can be used as stand-alone items, rather than having to use Safari to access the site. Look for apps for your favorite websites in the App Store, as a shortcut for accessing them quickly.

The iPhone 8 Plus also has a setting for **Show Tab Bar**, which displays the open tabs along the top of the Safari window, if the iPhone 8 Plus is being used in landscape mode.

Web Browsing with Safari

To start browsing the web with Safari and enjoy the variety of the information within it:

1 Tap once on the **Safari** app

2 Enter a website address here in the Address Bar, or tap once on one of the items in the Favorites window

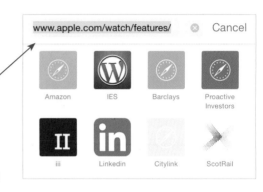

Don't forget

The **Share** button in Step 5 can be used to share a web page via Message, Mail or social media sites such as Facebook or Twitter. It can also be used to add a web page link to a Note.

3 As you type in the Address Bar, website suggestions appear, and also search suggestions with Google

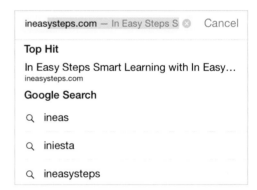

4 When you access a web page, use these buttons to visit the Next and Previous pages

5 Use this button to share a web page

6 Use this button to view bookmarks

7 Use this button to view, add and delete tabs (see pages 104-105)

Adding bookmarks

Everyone has favorite websites that they visit, and in Safari it is possible to mark these with bookmarks so that they can be accessed quickly. To do this:

1 Tap once on this button on the bottom toolbar

2 Tap once on the **Add Bookmark** button

Add Bookmark

3 Select a name and location for the bookmark, and tap once on the **Save** button

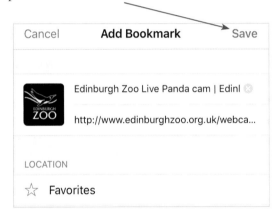

4 Tap once on the **Bookmarks** button, and tap once here to view your bookmarks

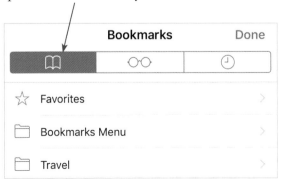

Hot tip

If the bottom toolbar is not visible on a web page, swipe downwards on the page to view it.

Don't forget

The **Bookmarks** button in Step 4 can also be used to access any Reading List items that have been stored. These are added from the **Share** button in Step 1, and enable items to be saved and read later, even if you are not connected to the internet. (The third button in Step 4 is for accessing your web browsing history.)

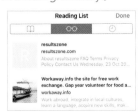

Using Tabs in Safari

In keeping with most modern web browsers, Safari uses tabs so that you can have several websites open at the same time. However, due the fact that a smartphone's screen is smaller than those on a desktop or laptop computer, tabs operate in a specific way on the iPhone. To use tabs:

1 Open Safari and open a website. Tap once on this button on the bottom toolbar to view all currently open tabs

2 Swipe up and down in Tab View to view all of the open tabs. Tap once on one to view that web page at full size

3 Swipe to the bottom of the page to view any tabs that you have open on any other Apple devices, such as an iPad

Hot tip

Press and hold on a tab to drag it into a different position in Tab View.

Press and hold the Tab button to 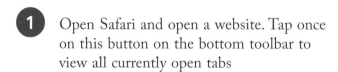 get the option to close all open tabs in one go.

Don't forget

Tap once on the **Done** button at the bottom of the Tab View window to exit this and return to the web page that was being viewed when Tab View was activated.

Opening tabs

To open more tabs in Safari on your iPhone:

1 Open the Tab View window as shown opposite, and tap once on this button

2 Open the new tab by entering a web address in the Address Bar, or by tapping once on one of the items in the Favorites window

The items that appear in the Favorites window can be specified with the Safari settings: **Settings** > **Safari** > **Favorites** and by then selecting a category. This page will appear when a new tab is opened, and also when you tap in the Address Bar to enter a web address.

3 Tap once on the **Private** button in Tab View to open a new tab that is not recorded in your web history

4 Open the private tab in the same way as a regular one. This is

indicated by a dark bar at the top of the window

5 Tap once on this button to close any tab in Tab View

Setting up an Email Account

Email accounts

Email settings can be specified within the Settings app. Different email accounts can also be added there.

1 Tap once on the **Settings** app

2 Tap once on the **Accounts & Passwords** tab

Accounts & Passwords

3 Tap once on the **Add Account** button to add a new account

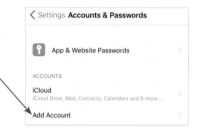

4 Tap once on the type of email account you want to add

Hot tip

If your email provider is not on the **Add Account** list, tap once on **Other** at the bottom of the list and complete the account details using the information from your email provider.

5 Enter the details for the account, and tap on the **Next** button to move through the wizard

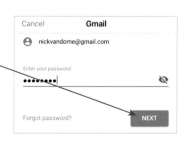

6 Drag these buttons **On** or **Off** to specify which functions are to be available for the required account. Tap once on the **Save** button

7 Each new account is added under the **Accounts** heading of the Mail section

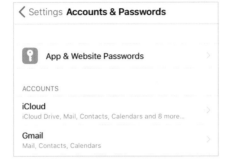

If you set up more than one email account, messages from all of them can be downloaded and displayed by **Mail**.

Email settings
Email settings can be specified within the Settings app:

1 Under the **Mail** section there are several options for how Mail operates and looks. These include how much of an email will be previewed in your Inbox, and options for accessing actions by swiping on an email

The **Organize by Thread** option can be turned **On** to show connected email conversations within your Inbox. If there is a thread of emails, this is indicated by this symbol.

Tap on it once to view the thread.

Emailing

Email on the iPhone is created, sent and received using the Mail app (although other mail apps can be downloaded from the App Store). This provides a range of functionality for managing emails and responding to them.

Accessing Mail

To access Mail and start sending and receiving emails:

1 Tap once on the **Mail** app (the red icon in the corner displays the number of unread emails in your Inbox)

2 Tap once on a message to display it in the main panel

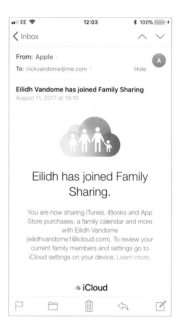

3 Use these buttons to, from left to right, flag a message, move a message to a specific folder, delete a message, respond to a message and create a new message

4 Tap once on this button to reply to a message, reply to everyone in a conversation, forward it to a new recipient, or print it

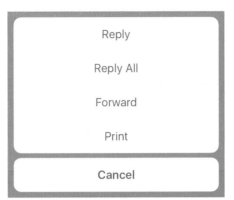

| Reply |
| Reply All |
| Forward |
| Print |
| Cancel |

Creating email

To create and send an email:

1 Tap once on this button to create a new message

2 Enter a recipient name in the **To:** box

Cancel	**Lunch**	Send

To: Eilidh Vandome

Cc/Bcc, From: nickvandome@me.com

Subject: Lunch

Hi, where would you like to go?

Sent from my iPhone

3 Enter a subject and body text

4 Tap once on the **Send** button to send the email to the recipient

Send

Having a Video Chat

Video chatting is a very personal and interactive way to keep in touch with family and friends around the world. The FaceTime app provides this facility with other iPhone, iPad and iPod Touch users, or a Mac computer with FaceTime. To use FaceTime for video chatting:

1 Tap once on the **FaceTime** app

2 Recent video chats are shown under the **Video** tab. Tap once here to select a contact

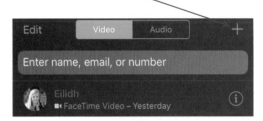

To make video calls with FaceTime you need an active internet connection and to be signed in with your Apple ID.

3 Tap once on a contact to access their details for making a FaceTime call

Skype is another option for making free video calls to other Skype users. The app can be downloaded from the App Store.

4 Tap once on their phone number or email address to make a FaceTime call. The recipient must have FaceTime on their iPhone, iPad, iPod Touch or Mac computer; or

5 Tap once on these buttons next to a contact to make a video or audio call

6 Once you have selected a contact, FaceTime starts connecting to

them and displays this at the top of the screen

7 When you have connected, your contact appears in the main window and you appear in a picture-in-picture thumbnail in the corner

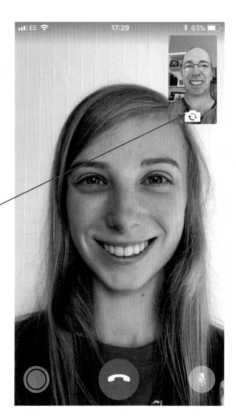

8 Tap once on this button on your own thumbnail photo to swap between cameras on your iPhone

Hot tip

The contacts for FaceTime calls are taken from the iPhone Contacts app. You can also add new contacts directly to the contacts list by tapping once on the **+** sign and adding the relevant details for the new contact.

111

9 Tap once on this button to take a Live Photo of the screen (this is a photo that is created as a small animation). Both devices require iOS 11 for this

NEW

Live Photos in FaceTime is a new feature in iOS 11 on the iPhone.

10 Tap once on this button to end the FaceTime call

Adding Social Media

Using social media sites such as Facebook, Twitter and Snapchat to keep in touch with family and friends has now become common across all generations. On the iPhone with iOS 11, it is possible to link to these accounts so that you can share content to them from your iPhone, and also view updates through the Notification Center. To add social media apps to your iPhone:

Hot tip

Updates can be set to appear in your **Notification Center**. Open **Settings**, and tap once on the **Notifications** tab. Under the **Notification Style** heading, tap once on the social media site and select options for how you would like the notifications to appear.

112

1 Open the App Store and navigate to the **Apps** > **Categories** > **Social Networking** section

Social Networking

2 Tap once on the required apps to download them to your iPhone

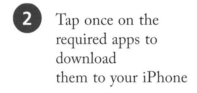

Don't forget

Social media sites can be accessed from their own apps on the iPhone, and also from their respective websites, using Safari.

3 Tap once on an app to open it

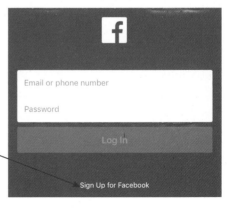

4 If you already have an account with the social media service, enter your login details, or tap once on the **Sign Up** button to create a new account

7 Hands on with Apps

Apps are the items that give the iPhone its functionality. This chapter details the pre-installed apps, and also shows how to access those in the App Store.

You need an active internet connection to download apps from the App Store.

Hot tip

Within a number of apps there is a **Share** button that can be used to share items through a variety of methods, including iMessages, email, Facebook and Twitter.

What is an App?

An app is just a more modern name for a computer program. Initially, it was used in relation to mobile devices such as the iPhone and the iPad, but it is now becoming more widely used with desktop and laptop computers, for both Mac and Windows operating systems.

On the iPhone there are two types of apps:

- **Pre-installed apps**. These are the apps that come already installed on the iPhone.

- **App Store apps**. These are apps that can be downloaded from the online App Store. There is a huge range of apps available there, covering a variety of different categories. Some are free, while others have to be paid for. The apps in the App Store are updated and added to on a daily basis, so there are always new ones to explore.

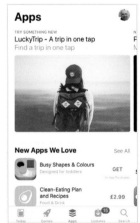

There are also two important points about apps (both pre-installed and those from the App Store) to remember:

- Apart from some of the pre-installed apps, the majority of apps do not interact with each other. This means that there is less chance of viruses being transmitted from app to app on your iPhone, and they can operate without a reliance on other apps.

- Content created by apps is saved within the app itself, rather than within a file structure on your iPhone; e.g. if you create a note in the Notes app, it is saved there; if you take a photo, it is saved in the Photos app. Content is usually also saved automatically when it is created or edited, so you do not have to worry about saving it as you work on it.

Pre-installed Apps

The pre-installed iPhone apps are the ones that appear on the Home screen when you first get your iPhone:

- **App Store**. This can be used to access the online App Store, from where additional apps can be downloaded and updated.

- **Calculator**. This is a basic calculator, which can also be accessed from the Control Center.

- **Calendar**. An app for storing appointments, important dates and other calendar information. It can be synced with iCloud.

- **Camera**. This gives direct access to the front-facing and rear-facing iPhone cameras.

- **Clock**. This displays the current time, and can be used to view the time in different countries. It also has an alarm clock and a stopwatch.

- **Compass**. This can be used to show you the direction of North. You can give the compass access to your location so that you can follow it from where you are.

- **Contacts**. An address book app. Once contacts are added here they can then also be accessed from other apps, such as Mail.

- **FaceTime**. This app uses the front-facing FaceTime camera to hold video or audio chats with compatible Apple devices.

- **Files**. This is used to back up items and make them available to other Apple devices.

Hot tip

Some of the default apps are located on the second Home screen, within the **Extras** folder.

Hot tip

If you don't want your contacts to be accessed by other apps then open **Settings** > **Privacy** > **Contacts** and drag the button for these apps to **Off**, if any appear here.

The Files app is a new feature in iOS 11.

...cont'd

- **Find Friends**. This can be used to view the location of family and friends, based on their Apple mobile devices and Mac computers.

- **Find iPhone**. This can be used to locate your iPhone and other Apple devices. It is set up in **Settings** > **iCloud**.

- **Health**. This stores and collates a range of health information. See pages 132-133.

- **Home**. This is a new app in iOS 11 that can be used to control certain compatible functions within the home, such as heating controls.

- **iBooks**. This is an app for downloading electronic books, which can then be read on the iPhone.

- **iTunes Store**. This app can be used to browse the iTunes Store, where content can be downloaded to your iPhone.

- **Mail**. This is the email app for sending and receiving email on your iPhone.

- **Maps**. Use this app to view maps from around the world, find specific locations, and get directions to destinations.

- **Messages**. This is the iPhone messaging service, which can be used for SMS text messages and iMessages between compatible Apple devices.

- **Music**. An app for playing music on your iPhone and also viewing cover artwork. You can also use it to create your own playlists.

- **News**. This collates news stories from numerous online publications and categories.

- **Notes**. If you need to jot down your thoughts or ideas, this app is perfect for just that.

Don't forget

You need an Apple ID to obtain content from the iTunes Store and iBooks.

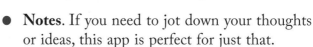

- **Photos**. This is an app for viewing and editing your photos and videos, and creating slideshows. It can also be used to share photos.

- **Podcasts**. This can be used to download podcasts from within the App Store.

- **Reminders**. Use this app to help keep organized, when you want to create to-do lists and set reminders for events.

- **Safari**. The Apple web browser that has been developed for viewing the web on your iPhone.

A podcast is an audio or video program, and they cover an extensive range of subjects.

- **Settings**. This contains a range of settings for the iPhone (see pages 20-21 for details).

- **Stocks**. Use this to display the latest stock market prices and add your own companies.

- **Tips**. This can be used to display tips and hints for items on your iPhone.

- **Videos**. This is an app for viewing videos from the iTunes Store, and also streaming them to a larger HDTV monitor.

- **Voice Memos**. This can be used to record short audio reminders that can be stored and played on the iPhone.

- **Wallet**. This can be used to store credit, debit and storecard details, for making payments with Apple Pay (in some locations).

- **Watch**. This can be used to pair an iPhone with the Apple Watch and apply a range of settings.

- **Weather**. Displays weather details for your location and destinations around the world.

About the App Store

While the pre-installed apps that come with the iPhone are flexible and versatile, apps really come into their own when you connect to the App Store. This is an online resource and there are thousands of apps there that can be downloaded and then used on your iPhone, including categories from Lifestyle to Medical and Travel.

To use the App Store, you must first have an Apple ID. This can be obtained when you first connect to the App Store. Once you have an Apple ID, you can start exploring the App Store and the apps within it:

Don't forget

The items within the Today section of the App Store change on a regular basis, so it is always worth looking at it from time to time.

1 Tap once on the **App Store** app on the Home screen

2 The latest available apps are displayed on the Homepage of the App Store, including the featured and best new apps

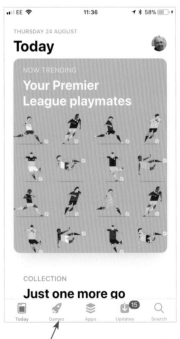

3 Tap on these buttons to view items according to **Today**, **Games**, **Apps**, and **Updates**

Viewing apps

To view apps in the App Store and read about their content
and functionality:

1 Tap once on an app

2 General details about
the app are displayed

3 Swipe left or
right here to
view additional
information about the
app, and view details

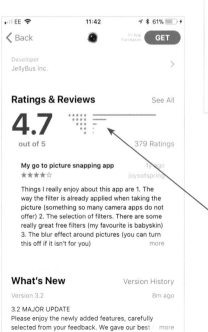

4 Reviews and
related apps are
available from the
relevant buttons,
next to the
Details button

Don't forget

If it is an upgraded
version of an app,
this page will include
details of any fixes and
improvements that
have been made.

Finding Apps

Featured

Within the App Store, apps are separated into categories according to type. This enables you to find apps according to particular subjects. To do this:

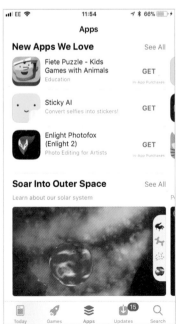

Some apps will differ depending on the geographical location from which you are accessing the App Store.

1 Tap once on the **Apps** button on the toolbar at the bottom of the App Store

2 Scroll up and down to view all of the sections within the Apps Homepage, and scroll left and right to view items within each section heading

3 Scroll up and down to view all of the sections within the Apps Homepage, and scroll left and right to view items within each section heading

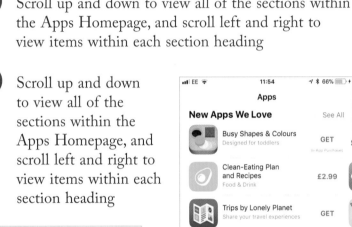

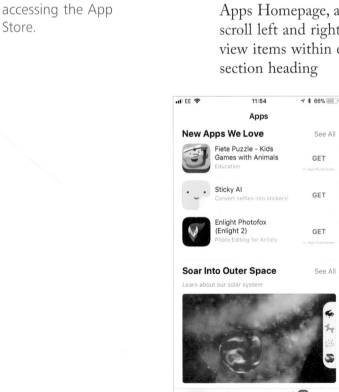

4 Scroll down the page to the **Top Categories** section, and tap once on the **See All** button to view the full range of categories of apps

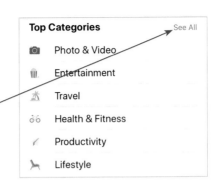

5 Tap once on a category to view the items within it. This can be navigated in the same way as the main Homepage in the App Store; e.g. swipe up and down to view sections, and left and right on each panel to view the available apps

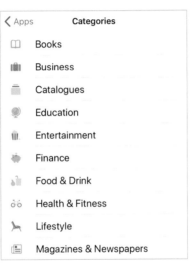

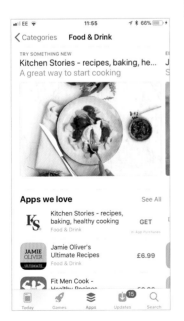

...cont'd

Top Charts
To find the top-rated apps:

1 Tap once on the **Apps** button on the toolbar at the bottom of the App Store

2 Scroll down the page to view the **Top Paid** and **Top Free** apps

3 Tap once on the **See All** button to view all of the Top Paid or Top Charts apps

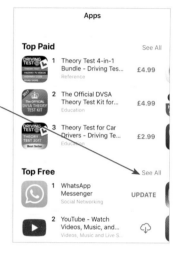

4 Tap once on the **All Apps** button

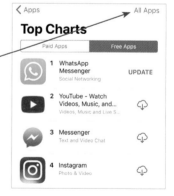

5 The top apps for that category are displayed

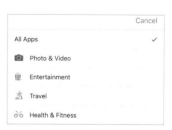

Searching for apps

Another way to find apps is with the App Store Search box, which appears at the top of the App Store window once it has been accessed. To use this to find apps:

1 Tap once on the **Search** button at the bottom of the window to access the Search box

2 Tap in the Search box to activate the keyboard and enter a search keyword or phrase

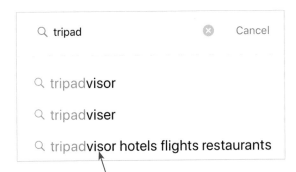

3 Suggested apps appear as you are typing

4 Tap on an app to view it

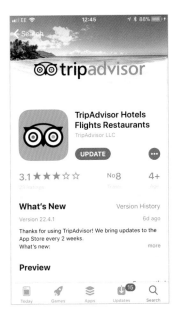

Don't forget

For more information about using the iPhone virtual keyboard, see Chapter 5.

123

Downloading Apps

When you identify an app that you would like to use, it can be downloaded to your iPhone. To do this:

Don't forget

Apps usually download in a few minutes or less, depending on the speed of your Wi-Fi connection.

1 Find the app you want, using the **App Store**

2 Tap once on the **Price** or **Get** button

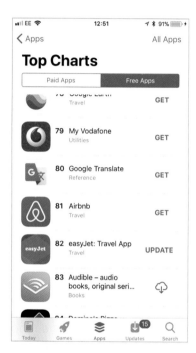

Beware

Some apps have "in-app purchases". This is additional content that has to be paid for when it is downloaded.

3 Tap once on the **Install** button

4 Enter the password for your Apple ID, and tap once on the **Sign In** button. The app will install

Updating Apps

The publishers of apps provide updates, which bring new features and improvements. You do not have to check your apps to see if there are updates – you can set them to be updated automatically through the Settings app. To do this:

1 Open **Settings** and tap on the **iTunes & App Store** tab

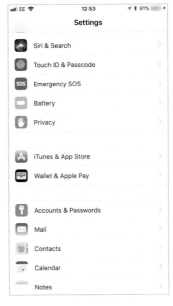

You should keep your apps as up-to-date as possible to take advantage of software fixes and any updates to the iPhone operating system (iOS).

2 Drag the **Updates** button under **Automatic Downloads** to **On** to enable automatic updates for apps

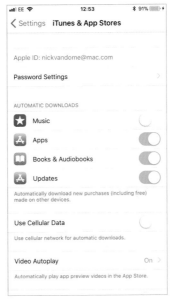

Managing your Apps

As more apps are added it can become hard to find the ones you want, particularly if you have to swipe between several screens. However, it is possible to organize apps into individual folders to make using them more manageable. To do this:

Hot tip

Folders are an excellent way to manage your apps, and ensure that you do not have numerous Home screens cluttered up with different apps.

Hot tip

Folders can also be added to the Dock after you have created them, enabling several apps to be stored here.

1 Press on an app until it starts to jiggle and a cross appears at the top-left corner. (The cross can be used to delete the app – see next page)

2 Drag the app over another one

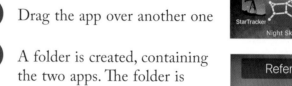

3 A folder is created, containing the two apps. The folder is given a default name, usually based on the category of the first app

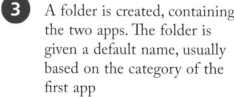

4 Tap once on the folder name and type a new name, if required

5 Tap on the **Done** button on the keyboard, or click on the **Home** button to finish creating the folder

6 Click the **Home** button again to return to the Home screen (this is done whenever you want to return to the Home screen from an app's folder)

7 The folder is added on the Home screen. Tap on this to access the items within it (press and hold on it to move it)

Deleting Apps

If you decide that you do not want certain apps anymore, they can be deleted from your iPhone. However, they remain in the iCloud so that you can reinstall them if you change your mind. This also means that if you delete an app by mistake, you can get it back from the App Store without having to pay for it again. To do this:

1 Press on an app until it starts to jiggle and a cross appears at the top-left corner

2 Tap once on the cross to delete the app. In the Delete dialog box, tap once on the **Delete** button

Delete "Hotels.com"?
Deleting this app will also delete its data, but any documents or data stored in iCloud will not be deleted.

Cancel	Delete

3 To reinstall a deleted app, tap once on the **App Store** app

4 Tap once on the **Updates** button on the bottom toolbar

If you delete an app it will also delete any data that has been compiled with that app, even if you reinstall it from the App Store.

Most of the pre-installed apps can now be deleted, using iOS 11. The ones that cannot be deleted are: App Store, Camera, Clock, Find iPhone, Health, Messages, Phone, Photos, Safari, Settings, and Wallet.

...cont'd

5 Tap once on account icon at the top of the window

6 Tap once on the **Purchased** button

7 Tap once on the **My Purchases** button to view all of your purchased apps

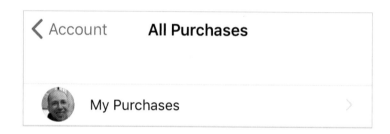

All of the apps that you have downloaded, including those on other Apple devices, will be listed in the My Purchases section of the App Store.

8 Tap once on the **iCloud** button to reinstall an app

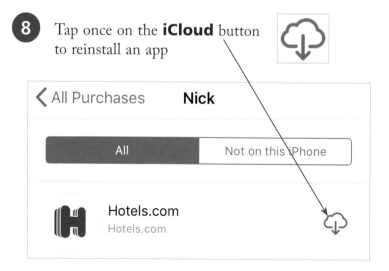

8 Apps for Every Day

The iPhone 8 has apps to make your day-to-day life run more efficiently and smoothly.

Health Options on the iPhone

The Health app

Health and general fitness is of interest to many of us, and the iPhone 8 recognizes this with a range

of apps designed to help us stay in good health and monitor our health activities. One way in which this is done is with the Health app. This can be used to store a range of health information, from how much sleep you get each night, to your cholesterol level. Data can be entered for regular time periods, and charts are produced for days, weeks, months and years. This enables you to build up an accurate picture of your health needs and activities. Other health apps can also communicate with the Health app so that more information can be aggregated.

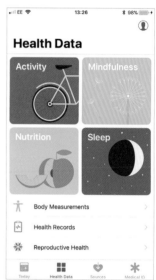

Don't forget

Wearable devices are beginning to capture the public's imagination and this will undoubtedly develop more in the future, particularly as they are used more in conjunction with body sensors, and health and fitness apps.

Working with the Apple Watch

In April 2015, Apple introduced the Apple Watch, followed by Apple Watch 2 in September 2016 and Apple Watch 3 in 2017. This is much more than a watch, though: it is also a body monitoring device. It has a number of sensors on the back, which monitor information such as heart rate and body movement. There is also an activity app to measure your fitness activities. A lot of this data can be sent to the Health app on the iPhone, where it can be stored and analyzed in greater depth. Wearable technology like the Apple Watch is undoubtedly a growth area, and there are likely to be more and more health and fitness features added as this technology evolves.

Don't forget

The Apple Watch has to be used in conjunction with an iPhone 6 (or later) to activate its full range of functionality. It is "paired" with an iPhone using the Watch app.

App Store health and fitness apps

The App Store not only has a wide range of health and fitness apps; it even has a whole category for them:

1 Tap once on the **App Store** app

2 Tap once on the **Apps** button

3 In the categories section, tap once on the **Health & Fitness** category

4 The health and fitness apps are displayed. Scroll down the page to view the **Top Paid** and **Top Free** health and fitness apps

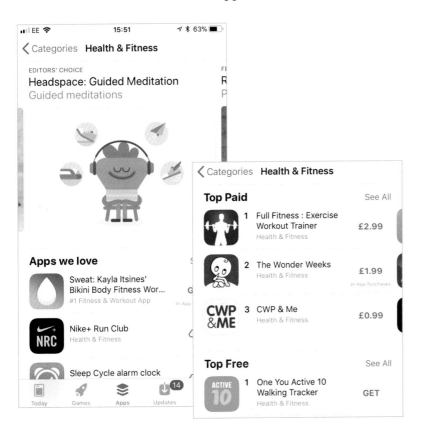

Beware

Some health and fitness apps are free, but they then offer in-app purchases for additional features.

Don't forget

The App Store also has a **Medical** category.

Beware

If you have a pre-existing medical condition, or are on any medication, always consult your doctor before using a new health or fitness app that could have an impact on this.

Using the Health App

The Health app is available in iOS 11, and it enables you to input and analyze a wide range of health and fitness information. There are four main areas:

Don't forget

New apps designed to interact with the Health app are being produced by a number of different third-party developers.

Hot tip

Tap on the calendar at the top of the Today window to view data from different dates. The current date is indicated by a red circle.

Don't forget

Some items in the Health app have data added automatically, such as Walking + Running, Steps, and Flights Climbed, in the Activity category. Other items need to have their data added manually (see next page).

- **Health Data**. This displays the available categories within the Health app.

- **Today**. This displays health data that has been collated for specific days.

- **Sources**. This displays information from any other health apps on your iPhone, providing they have requested access to the Health app.

- **Medical ID**. This can be used to add your own medical information such as medical conditions, allergies, blood type and emergency contacts.

Adding health data

To enter a range of information into the Health app:

1 Tap once on the **Health Data** button

2 Tap once on one of the main categories

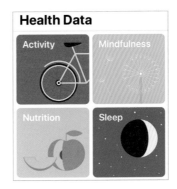

3 Tap once on one of the sub-categories, e.g. Calcium in the Nutrition category

4 Tap once on this button to add data for the selected item

5 Add the data for the selected item, and tap once on the **Add** button

Don't forget

Here, you get the option to enter your personal data and medical details. It is well worth entering these for emergencies.

Beware

When adding data, do so at regular intervals, otherwise the results and analysis may not be complete.

Don't forget

Once data has been added, it is shown on the graph in Step 4. Add data for more categories, as required.

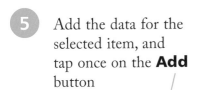

Hot tip

See **iPhone & Apple Watch for Health & Fitness in easy steps** for more help on using these devices to achieve your health goals.

Jotting Down Notes

It is always useful to have a quick way of making notes of everyday things, such as shopping lists, recipes or packing lists for traveling. On your iPhone, the Notes app is perfect for this function. To use it:

Don't forget

If iCloud is turned **On** for Notes (**Settings > Apple ID > iCloud > Notes**) then all of your notes will be stored here and will be available on any other iCloud-enabled devices that you have.

Don't forget

The first line of a note becomes its title when viewed in the list of all notes. (To view this, tap once on the **iCloud** button in Step 3.)

Don't forget

You can edit a note at any time by tapping on it once in the top-level folder and editing the text as required.

1 Tap once on the **Notes** app

2 Tap once on this button on the bottom toolbar to create a new note

3 Enter text for the note

4 Tap once on this button to share (via Message or Mail, or any social media apps on your iPhone), copy or print a note

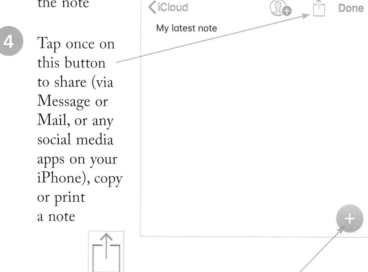

5 Tap once on this button to access the formatting toolbar (Tap once on the cross to close the toolbar.)

6 Double-tap on text to select it, and tap once on this button to access text formatting options

For more information about selecting text, see pages 84-85.

7 Tap once on this button to create a checklist. Add items to the list. Tap once on a check button to add a tick and show it as completed

Hot tip

Press and hold firmly on the keyboard in Notes to activate it as a trackpad. You can then swipe over it to move the cursor around the screen. This can also be done in the Mail and Messages apps.

8 Tap once on this button to share the current note and allow someone else to edit it

9 Select how you want to share the note, e.g. Message, Mail or a social media app

10 Enter any additional text as required, and send the message. The recipient will then be able to access the note and edit it (if they have a compatible device)

Don't forget

Tap once on this icon on the bottom toolbar to delete the current note.

...cont'd

11 Tap once on this button to add a handwritten item or drawing

12 Select a drawing object at the bottom of the screen, and draw on the screen. Tap once on the **Done** button. The drawing is added to the current note

Tap once on the **Scan Documents** button in Step 13 to scan a document into the current note. This is a new feature in iOS 11 on the iPhone.

13 Tap once on this button to add a photo or video to a note. Select a photo or video from your library, or take a new one

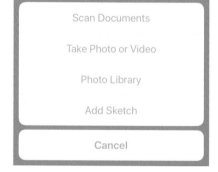

14 The latest note appears at the top of the iCloud list. Each time a note is edited, it moves to the top

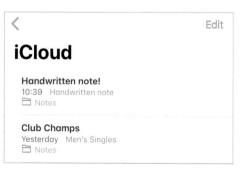

Keeping Up-to-Date

The Calendar can be used to add events and appointments and keep yourself up-to-date with your daily, monthly and annual activities.

1   Tap once on the **Calendar** app

2   If **Month** view is displayed, tap once here to access **Year** view. In Year view, tap once on a month to view it

3   Tap once on a day to view it (the current day is highlighted red)

Hot tip

Tap once on the **Today** button from any date to view the current date, in whichever view you are currently in.

137

4   Swipe up and down to view any events in **Day** view. Tap once on an event to view its details

...cont'd

Adding events

To add new events to the calendar:

Hot tip

Drag the **All-day** button to **On** to set an event for the whole day, rather than adding specific start and end times.

Don't forget

The repeat frequency for an event can be set to every day, every week, every 2 weeks, every month or every year. There is also a **Custom** option for specific time periods.

1 Press and hold on a timeslot within Day view, or tap once on this button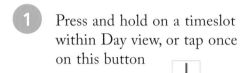

2 Enter a title for the event, and tap once on the **Starts** button to add a start time

3 Add an end time, by tapping on the **Ends** button, and also a repeat frequency (for recurring events such as birthdays). Select a specific calendar for the event and add an alert, if required. Tap once on the **Add** button to create the event

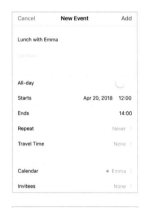

4 Tap once on this button to view a list of your current events and appointments

Getting the News

The iPhone with iOS 11 is ideal for keeping up with the news, whether you are on the move or at home. This is made even easier with the News app, which can be used to collate news stories from numerous online media outlets, covering hundreds of subjects. To use it:

1 Tap once on the **News** app

2 Tap once on the **Search** button to select topics to populate the news feed

3 Tap once on the heart icon on an item to follow it and add it to the news feed

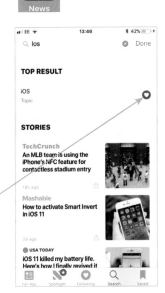

4 Tap once on the **Following** button on the bottom toolbar to view the publications that were added in Step 3

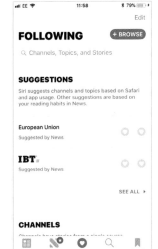

> **Hot tip**
>
> To delete an item from the Following section, tap once on the **Edit** button in the top right-hand corner and tap on the red circle next to the item you want to delete. This will remove its related content from your news feed.

...cont'd

5 Tap once on the **For You** button to view the news feed from selected publications and subjects. Tap here to view the full selection for the main heading (e.g. Top Stories)

For You

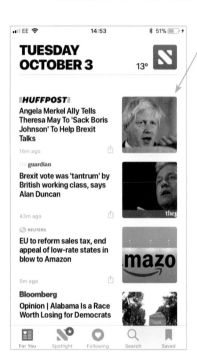

6 Scroll down the main For You page to view top-trending topics within the News app

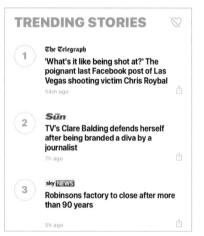

7 When an article has been opened for reading, tap on these buttons on the top toolbar to, from left to right: share the item (or save it), unfollow a news topic so you see fewer items, or follow a news topic for more similar items

9 Relaxing with your iPhone

This chapter shows how to get the most out of your iPhone for playing music and reading, and also how to shop and research online.

Around the iTunes Store

The iPhone performs an excellent role as a mobile entertainment center: its versatility means that you can carry your music, videos and books in your pocket. Most of this content comes from the online iTunes Store. To access this and start adding content to your iPhone:

Don't forget

Tap once on the **Genres** button at the top of the Music Homepage to view items for different musical genres and styles.

Don't forget

Tap once on the **Charts** tab at the top of the iTunes Store window to view the top-ranking items for the category that is being viewed.

1 Tap once on the **iTunes Store** app

2 The iTunes Store interface is similar to the App Store. Tap once on the **Featured** or **Charts** tabs at the top of the window to view these headings

3 Use the buttons on the bottom toolbar to access content for Music, Films/Movies and TV Programmes/Shows

4 Swipe to the left and right on each panel to view items within it

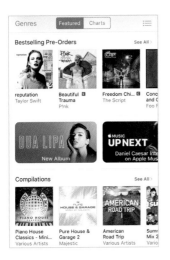

5 Swipe up and down to view more headings

Beware

Downloaded movies and TV shows take up a lot of storage space on the iPhone.

6 Tap once on the **Films/Movies** button to view the movies in the iTunes Store. These can be bought or rented

7 Tap once on the **TV Programmes/Shows** button to view the TV shows in the iTunes Store. These can be bought or rented

8 Tap once on the **More** button to access additional content

9 Tap once on the **Genius** button to view suggested content, based on what you have already bought from the iTunes Store

Don't forget

To view all of your iTunes purchases, tap once on the **More** button on the bottom toolbar and tap once on the **Purchased** button. View your purchases by category (Music, Films/Movies or TV Programmes/Shows), and tap once on the cloud symbol next to a purchased item to download it to your iPhone.

Buying Items

Once you have found the content you want in the iTunes Store, you can then buy it and download it to your iPhone.

Don't forget

If you have set up Apple Pay (see pages 48-49) you will be able to use this to buy items in the iTunes Store. Use the Touch ID function (see page 25) in Step 1, after you have tapped on the price button, to authorize the payment using Apple Pay.

 For music items, tap once on the price button next to an item (either an album or individual songs) and follow the instructions. Tap once on the **Music** app to play the item (see next page)

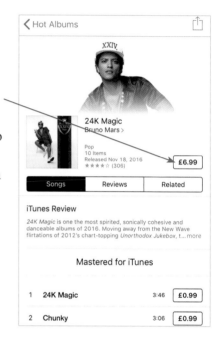

Don't forget

For rented movies and TV shows, you have 30 days to watch an item after you have downloaded it. After you have started watching, you have 48 hours until it expires.

 For movies and TV shows, tap once on the **Buy** or **Rent** button next to the title. Tap once on the **Videos** app to play the item

Playing Music

Once music has been bought from the iTunes Store, it can be played on your iPhone using the Music app. To do this:

1 Tap once on the **Music** app

2 Tap once on the **Library** button on the bottom toolbar

3 Select one of the options for viewing items in the Library. This can be **Playlists**, **Artists**, **Albums**, **Songs** and **Downloaded Music**

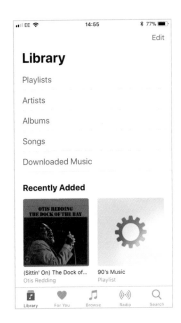

Hot tip

To create a playlist of songs, tap once on the **Playlists** button in Step 3, then tap once on the **New Playlist...** button. Give it a name and then add songs from your Library, using the **Add Music** button.

145

4 For the **Artists** section, tap once on an artist to view details of their songs on your iPhone

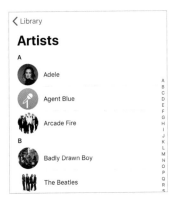

...cont'd

Don't forget

Tap once on this button in Step 5 to access a menu for the current track. This includes options to download the track, delete it from the Music app Library, add it to a playlist, or add it to the queue of music to be played.

Don't forget

By default, music that has been bought from the iTunes Store is kept online and can be played on your iPhone by streaming it over Wi-Fi. However, it is also possible to download tracks to your iPhone so that you can play them without being online. Tap once on this button to download a specific track.

5 Select a track to play it

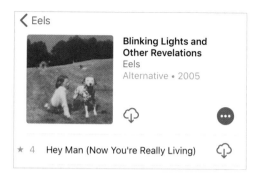

6 A limited version of the music controls appears at the bottom of the window

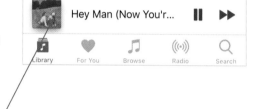

7 Tap once here to view the full version of the music controls. Use these buttons to return to the start of a track, play/pause a track, fast-forward, and adjust the volume

Using Apple Music

Apple Music is a service that makes the entire Apple iTunes Library of music available to users. It is a subscription service, but there is a three-month free trial. Music can be streamed over the internet or downloaded so you can listen to it when you are offline. To start with Apple Music:

1 Tap once on the **Music** app

2 Tap once on the **For You** button

3 Tap once on the **Choose Your Plan** button. (This option is available if you have already used the free, three-month trial of Apple Music)

4 Select the type of plan to which you want to subscribe and tap once on the **Join Apple Music** button. Once you have joined Apple Music, you will be able to select the music genres in which you are most interested and receive suggestions based on this. You will also be able to listen to the entire iTunes Library of music

To end your Apple Music subscription at any point (and to ensure you do not subscribe at the end of the free trial) open the **Settings** app. Tap once on the **iTunes & App Store** button, and tap once on your own **Apple ID** link (in blue). Tap once on the **View Apple ID** button and enter your Apple ID password. Under **Subscriptions**, tap once on the **Manage** button. Drag the **Automatic Renewal** button to **Off**. You can then renew your Apple Music membership, if required, by selecting one of the **Renewal Options**. If you do not renew your subscription once the free trial finishes, you will not be able to access any music that you have downloaded during the trial.

Reading

In addition to audio and visual content from the iTunes Store, it is also possible to read books on your iPhone, using the iBooks app. To do this:

1 Tap once on the **iBooks** app

2 Tap once on the **My Books** button on the bottom toolbar to view any items you have in your Library

Although not as large as a book, or an electronic book reader, both the iPhone 8 and iPhone 8 Plus are acceptable for reading books. The larger iPhone 8 Plus is the better option, but the high-quality Retina screen on both models means that it is an option for reading, particularly if you are traveling.

3 If a title has a cloud icon next to it, tap once on this to download the book to your iPhone

4 Tap once on the **Featured** button on the bottom toolbar to view books in the iBooks Store

5 The **Featured** interface of the iBooks Store is similar to that for the iTunes Store. Swipe up and down, or left and right, to view the content in the iBooks Store. Tap once on the **Top Charts** button on the bottom toolbar to view the top-selling titles in different categories

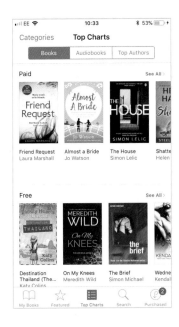

If you have a Kindle account, you can download the Kindle app from the App Store and use this to connect to your account and all of the books within it.

6 Once books have been downloaded to your iPhone, tap once on a title in the **My Books** section to read it. Tap on the left or right of the screen to move between pages, or swipe from the left or right edges. Tap in the middle of a page to activate the reading controls at the top of the screen, including table of contents, text size, and color options

Shopping

Online shopping was one of the first great commercial successes on the web. Thousands of retailers now have their own websites and, increasingly, their own apps that can be used on the iPhone. So there are now more options than ever for online shopping:

Don't forget

For some online retailers, you will have to register and create an account before you can buy items. For others, you will be able to go straight to the checkout and enter your payment details.

Don't forget

A number of online retailers offer Apple Pay (see pages 48-49) as a method of payment, denoted by the Apple Pay logo. The number of retailers offering this is likely to grow considerably as Apple Pay becomes more widely available.

1 Download apps from the App Store for well-known retailers such as Amazon and eBay

2 Use Safari and look up the retailer's website (in some cases, the website will have an option to download the app too)

3 For some websites, they will only enable you to download the retailer's app and use this

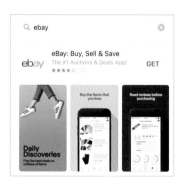

Comparing prices

Online retailing has also made it a lot easier to compare prices between sites. This can be done in two main ways:

1 Use Safari and search for price comparison websites. Different sites specialize in different products and services, so you may want to use a number of them

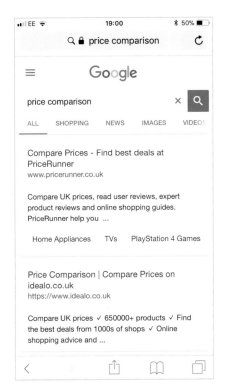

Another option for comparing prices is to check them in a bricks-and-mortar shop and then compare them with the online prices.

2 There are apps in the App Store that can be used to scan barcodes of products and then compare prices for a specific item across different retailers

Researching

With your iPhone in your hand, you literally have a world of information at your fingertips. Whatever your hobby or interest, you will be able to find out a lot more about it using several different options:

1 Press and hold on the **Home** button to access **Siri** and make an enquiry this way

2 Use the **App Store** to search for apps for your chosen subject

Don't forget

By default, the search engine used by Safari is Google. However, this can be changed in **Settings** > **Safari** > **Search Engine**.

3 Search **Safari** to find related websites and also general information about a specific topic

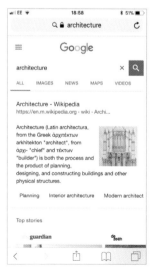

10 On the Go

The iPhone 8 is a great companion whenever you are out and about anywhere, whether at home or abroad.

Finding Locations

Finding locations around the world is only ever a couple of taps away when you have your iPhone and the Maps app.

154

1 Tap once on the **Maps** app

2 The Search box is at the bottom of the window

3 Enter an item into the Search box. As you type, suggestions appear underneath. Tap on one to go to that location

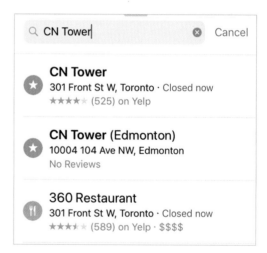

4 For the current location, options for searching over items such as food outlets, shops and entertainment are available. Tap on one of these to see results for these categories in the current location

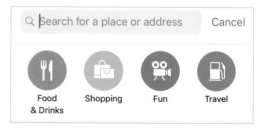

5 The location selected in Step 3 is displayed, with information about it at the bottom of the window

Some locations, such as airports and shopping centers, can display indoor layouts. This is a new feature in iOS 11 on the iPhone.

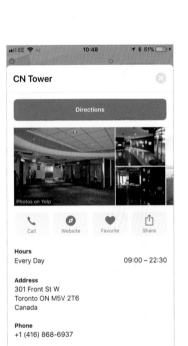

6 Swipe up from the bottom of the window to view full details about the location, including photos, address, phone number and website address, if available

Hot tip

Some locations have a 3D Flyover Tour feature. This is an automated tour of a location, featuring its most notable sites. It covers major cities around the world, and the list is regularly being added to. If it is available for a location, tap once on the **Flyover** button at the bottom of the window, next to the **Directions** button. Try it with a location such as New York, London or Paris.

7 At the top of the Maps app window, tap once on this icon for map style options (i)

8 Select either **Standard (Map)**, **Transit** or **Satellite** to view the map in that style

Getting Directions

Wherever you are in the world, you can get directions between two locations. To do this:

You can enter the Start point as your current location. Tap once on this button to view your current location.

If you enter the name of a landmark you may also be shown other items that have the same name, such as businesses.

For some destinations, alternative routes will be displayed, depending on distance and traffic conditions. Tap once on the alternative route to select it. Directions for each route can be selected at the bottom of the window.

1 Tap once in the Search box at the bottom of the window in the Maps app

2 Enter the destination (by default, this is from your current location)

3 Tap once on the **Directions** button. The route is shown on the map

Blairgowrie Rugby Club
17 mi

Directions
33 min drive

Address
Coupar Angus Road
Blairgowrie
PH10
Scotland

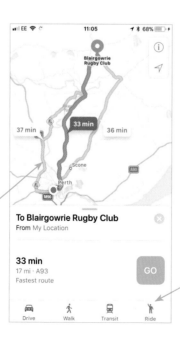

4 Tap once on these buttons at the bottom of the window to view the route for **Drive**, **Walk**, **Transit** or a taxi **Ride** using an appropriate app

5 Tap once on the **Go** button to view step-by-step instructions on the map

6 The route is displayed, from your starting location. Audio instructions tell you the directions to be followed. You can use the volume buttons (on the side) to increase or decrease the sound. As you follow the route, the map and instructions are updated

Don't forget

The arrow in Step 6 points in the current direction of travel.

7 Swipe up from the bottom of the screen to access options for viewing items such as gas stations and food outlets on the route. These are displayed on the map, in relation to the current route being followed

Don't forget

Tap once on the **End** button and then the **End Route** button to stop following the current route.

Booking a Trip

Most major travel retailers have had their own websites for a number of years. They have now moved into the world of apps, and these can be used on your iPhone to book almost any type of vacation, from cruises to city breaks.

Several apps for the iPhone (and their associated websites) offer full travel services where they can deal with flights, hotels, insurance, car hire and excursions. These include:

- **Expedia**
- **Kayak**
- **Orbitz**
- **Travelocity**

These apps usually list special offers and last-minute deals on their Homepages, and they offer options for booking flights, hotels, car hire and activities separately.

Hot tip

It is always worth searching different apps to get the best possible price. In some cases, it is cheapest to buy different elements of a vacation from different retailers, e.g. flights from one seller and accommodation from another.

Don't forget

Most travel apps have specific versions based on your geographical location. You will be directed to these by default.

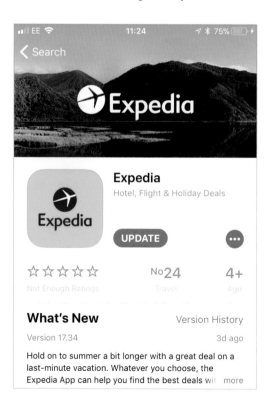

TripAdvisor

One of the best resources for travelers is TripAdvisor. Not only does the app provide a full range of opportunities for booking flights and hotels; it also has an extensive network of reviews from people who have visited the countries, hotels and restaurants on the site. These are independent, and usually very fair and honest. In a lot of cases, if there are issues with a hotel or restaurant, the proprietor posts a reply to explain what is being done to address any problems.

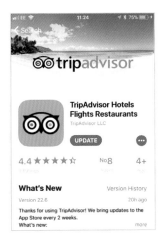

TripAdvisor has a certain sense of community, so post your own reviews once you have been places, to let others know about your experience.

Cruises

There are also apps dedicated specifically to cruises. One to look at is iCruise, which searches over a range of companies for your perfect cruise.

Booking Hotels

The internet is a perfect vehicle for finding good-value hotel rooms around the world. When hotels have spare capacity, this can quickly be relayed to associated websites and apps, where users can often benefit from cheap prices and special offers. There are plenty of apps that have details of thousands of hotels around the world, such as:

Trivago

An app that searches over one million hotels on more than 250 sites, to ensure you get the right hotel for the best price.

Hotels.com

A stylish app that enables you to enter search keywords into a Search box on the Home screen to find hotels based on destination, name or local landmarks.

Hot tip

Most hotel apps have reviews of all of the listed establishments. It is always worth reading these, as it gives you a view from the people who have actually been there.

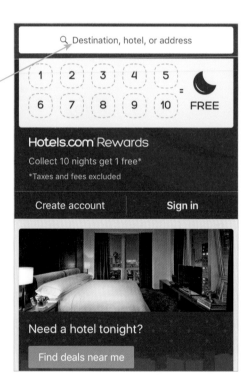

Booking.com

Another good, fully-featured hotel app that provides a comprehensive service and excellent prices.

LateRooms.com

An app that specializes in getting the best prices by dealing with rooms that are available at short notice. Some genuine bargains can be found here, for hotels of all categories.

Hot tip

Currency converters can also be downloaded from the App Store so that you can see how much your money is worth in different countries.

Finding Flights

Flying is a common part of modern life and although you do not have to book separate flights for a vacation (if it is part of a package), there are a number of apps for booking flights and also for following the progress of those in the air:

Skyscanner

This app can be used to find flights at airports around the world. Enter your details such as leaving airport, destination and dates of travel. The results show a range of available options, covering different price ranges and airlines.

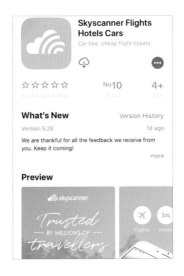

Flight apps need to have an internet connection in order to show real-time flight information.

Flightradar24

If you like viewing the path of flights that are in the air, or need to check if flights are going to be delayed, this app provides this inflight information. Flights are shown according to flight number and airline.

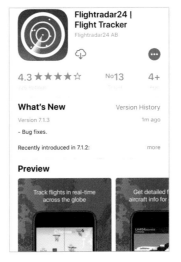

FlightAware Flight Tracker

Another app for tracking flights, showing arrivals and departures and also information about delays. It can track commercial flights worldwide.

Speaking Their Language

When you are traveling abroad, it is always beneficial to learn some of the language of the country you are visiting. With your iPhone at hand this has become a whole lot easier, and there are a number of options:

There are also some keyboard translator apps in the App Store that can be used to translate items that you receive in any app. One to look at is **Keyboard plus language translation**.

1 Translation apps that can be used to translate words, phrases and sentences in every language you probably need

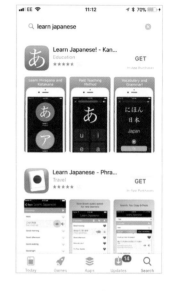

2 Language apps that offer options in several languages

Some language apps are free, but they then charge for additional content, known as in-app purchases.

3 Specific language apps, where you can fully get to grips with a new language

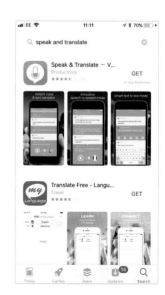

11 Camera and Photos

The iPhone 8 has a high-quality camera and the Photos app for viewing your photos.

The iPhone Camera

Because of its mobility and the quality of the screen, the iPhone is excellent for taking and displaying photos and videos. Photos can be captured directly using one of the two built-in cameras (one on the front and one on the back) and then viewed, edited and shared using the Photos app. To do this:

1 Tap once on the **Camera** app

2 Select the Photo option and tap once on this button to capture a photo

3 Tap once on this button to swap between the front or back cameras on the iPhone

The iPhone cameras can be used for different formats. Swipe left or right just above the shutter button, to access the different shooting options:

1 Tap once on the **Square** button to capture photos at this ratio

2 Tap once on the **Video** button and press the red shutter button to take a video

3 Tap once on the **Time-lapse** button and press the shutter button (which appears in red with a ring around it) to create
a time-lapse image: the camera keeps taking photos periodically until you press the shutter button again

Don't forget

The camera on the back of the iPhone 8 is a 12-megapixel iSight one, and is capable of capturing high-resolution photos and also high definition and 4K videos. The front-facing one is a 7-megapixel one, and is excellent for video calls using FaceTime.

Don't forget

When a video has been captured it is stored within the **Photos** app.

164

4 Tap once on the **Slo-Mo** button and press the red shutter button to take a slow-motion video

5 Tap once on the **Pano** button to create a panoramic image

Don't forget

The iPhone 8 Plus has a dual-lens iSight camera, using a telephoto lens and a wide-angle one, for additional versatility when taking photos.

6 Move the iPhone slowly to the right to create the panorama. Each photo will be taken automatically when the camera is in the correct position

7 Tap once on the **Portrait** button to capture options for portrait shots (see page 166 for details)

Hot tip

To take a quick photo, open the **Camera** app and press on either of the volume buttons.

Camera functions

The buttons at the top of the camera window can be used to create additional functionality.

1 Tap once on the **Flash** button to set it for **Auto**, **On** or **Off**

2 Tap once on the **Self-timer** button to set it for **Off**, **3s** or **10s**

3 Tap once on this button to add a filter effect before you take a photo (see page 167)

Don't forget

Tap once on this button on the top toolbar to turn it yellow, to take a Live Photo (see page 168).

165

...cont'd

Portrait mode

Taking photos of people is one of the most common uses for the iPhone's camera. This is enhanced by Portrait mode, which creates a photo with a slightly blurred background, so that the main subject stands out more. It can also be used to change the lighting of the photo. To do this:

Portrait mode has been enhanced in iOS 11 on the iPhone 8.

Portrait mode can only be used with the main iPhone camera (the front-facing one).

1   Select the **Portrait** shooting option as shown on page 165

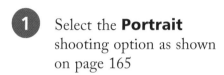

2   The lighting options are shown above the **Portrait** button. Tap once on the current selection to access the other options. Swipe on the arc to move between the options

3   For the **Stage Light** option, there is a circle into which the subject can be placed to ensure the best lighting is applied in this area

Camera filters

The camera on the iPhone 8 can be used to apply a range of vibrant, but subtle, filter effects when photos are taken:

1. Tap once on the **Filters** button as shown on page 165

The filter effects have been enhanced in iOS 11 on the iPhone 8.

2. The filter effects appear at the bottom of the window. If no effect has been applied, **Original** is the selection

3. Swipe along the Filters bar to view the options. Tap once on one to apply it to the photo

When a filter effect has been selected, this button is displayed in the top right-hand corner of the camera window. It remains active until it is turned off. To do this, tap once on the button to access the filters, and tap once on **Original**.

167

...cont'd

The Live Photo effects (Loop, Bounce and Long Exposure) are a new feature in iOS 11 on the iPhone 8.

The **Loop** option creates a continuous loop of the animated effect; the **Bounce** option plays and rewinds the Live Photo continuously; and the **Long Exposure** option can be used where most of the image is static and there is one moving element, such as flowing water. Tap once on each option to apply it to the Live Photo: the selected option is denoted in the top left-hand corner of the photo.

Live Photos

One feature on the camera is the Live Photos functionality. This enables you to take what seems like a single photo, but it creates an animated photo, which is actually a short video clip. To take Live Photos:

1 Tap once on this button on the top toolbar until it turns yellow, and **Live** appears. Take the photo using the **Photo** button, making sure that it includes some movement

2 Tap on the thumbnail of the photo in the bottom left corner to open it in the **Photos** app, then press and hold on it to view the animated effect. The word **Live** in the top left-hand corner identifies its type

3 Swipe up on the Live Photo to access options for editing it. These include **Loop** and **Bounce**

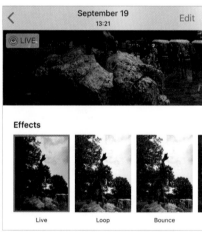

4 Swipe from right to left to access the third option, which is **Long Exposure**

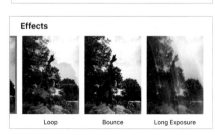

Photo Settings

iCloud sharing

Certain camera options can be applied within Settings. Several of these are to do with storing and sharing your photos via iCloud. To access these:

1 Tap once on the **Settings** app

2 Tap once on the **Photos** tab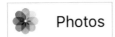

3 Drag the **iCloud Photo Library** button to **On** to upload your whole iPhone photo library to the iCloud. You will then be able to access this from any other Apple devices that you have. Similarly, photos on your other Apple devices can also be uploaded to the iCloud, and these will be available on your iPhone (requires other devices to be running iOS 8, or later, for mobile Apple devices or OS X Yosemite, or later, for desktop or laptop ones)

4 Drag the **Upload to My Photo Stream** button to **On** to enable all new photos and videos from your iPhone to be uploaded automatically to iCloud

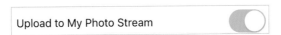

5 Drag the **iCloud Photo Sharing** button to **On** to allow you to create albums within the Photos app that can then be shared with other people via iCloud

Don't forget

Drag the **Grid** button in the **Camera** settings to **On** to place a grid over the screen when you are taking photos with the camera, if required. This can be used to help compose photos by placing subjects using the grid.

Viewing Photos

Once photos have been captured, they can be viewed and organized in the Photos app. To do this:

1 Tap once on the **Photos** app

2 At the top level, all photos are displayed according to the years in which they were taken

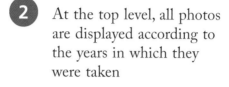

3 Tap once within the **Years** window to view photos according to specific, more defined, timescales and locations. This is the **Collections** level. Tap once on the **Years** button to move back up one level

4 Tap once within the **Collections** window to drill down further into the photos, within the **Moments** window. Tap once on the **Collections** button to go back up one level

Don't forget

Moments are created according to the time at which the photos were added or taken: photos added at the same time will be displayed within the same Moment.

5 Tap once on a photo within the **Moments** window to view it at full size. Tap once here to go back up one level

Hot tip

Double-tap with one finger on a full-size photo to zoom in on it. Double-tap with two fingers again to zoom back out. To zoom in to a greater degree, swipe outwards with thumb and forefinger. To zoom back out, pinch inwards with thumb and forefinger.

6 Swipe left and right to move through all of the available full-size photos in a specific Moment

...cont'd

Viewing Memories

The Photos app also has a section where the best of your photos are selected and displayed automatically. To use this:

1 Tap once on the **Memories** button on the bottom toolbar

2 The Photos app automatically collates photos into groups of Memories, based on criteria such as location, people or **Best of Last 3 Months**. Tap once on a Memory to view the photos within it

172

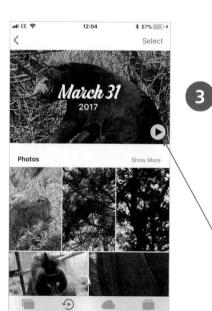

3 The Photos app selects what it considers the best photos for each Memory, and displays them on the page. Swipe down the page to view the photos. It also creates a movie (slideshow). Tap once here to view the movie

4 The Memories movie shows the photos in a variety of formats to give an attractive display

5 Tap once on a movie as it is playing to view the timeline at the bottom of the screen and also settings to customize the slideshow

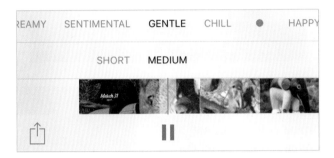

Options for customizing a Memories movie include the style, which determines the title style and transitions between photos and the overall speed of the movie.

6 Swipe down to the bottom of the Memory in Step 3 to view a map with the locations of the photos and also related Memories, based on similar locations and people

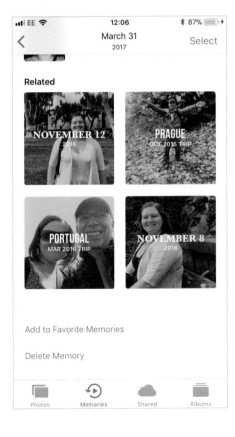

Tap once on the **Edit** button at the top of the window when a Memories movie is playing, as shown in Step 5 to access more Settings for a movie, including editing the title, adding music and adding more photos.

Editing Photos

The Photos app has options to perform some basic photo-editing operations. To use these:

1 Open a photo at full-screen size and tap once on this button to access the editing tools, on the bottom toolbar

2 Tap once on the **Enhance** button to have auto-coloring editing applied to the photo

3 Tap once on the **Crop** button and drag the resizing handles to select an area of the photo that you want to keep, and click **Done** to discard the rest

4 From the Crop section, tap once on the **Rotate** button to rotate the photo 90 degrees at a time, anti-clockwise

5 Tap once on the **Filters** button to select special effects to be applied to the photo

6 Tap once on the **Exposure** button to enable manual color editing for different options

Hot tip

If you reopen a photo that has been edited and closed, you have an option to **Revert** to its original state, before it was edited.

7 For each function, tap once on the **Done** button to save the photo with the selected changes

8 Tap once on the **Cancel** button to quit the editing process

Adding Albums

Albums can be used in the Photos app to store photos for different events or categories.

176

Don't forget

Photos can be selected in the same way as in Step 4 and used in other ways, too. For instance, they can be selected and then shared with other people, using the **Share** button; or deleted, using the **Trash** button.

Don't forget

Tap once on the **Shared** button on the bottom toolbar of the Photos app to create albums, which can then be shared with other people. Tap once on this button in the Shared section to create a new album for sharing.

1 Open the **Photos** app and tap once on the **Albums** button on the bottom toolbar

Albums

2 Tap once on this button to create an album

$+$

3 Give the album a name and tap once on the **Save** button

New Album
Enter a name for this album.

Gardens

Cancel   Save

4 In the Moments section, tap once on the top **Select** button to select all the items in a Moment

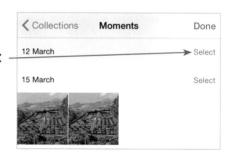

‹ Collections   **Moments**   Done
12 March   Select
15 March   Select

5 Tap on any individual photos to deselect them, and then tap once on the **Done** button

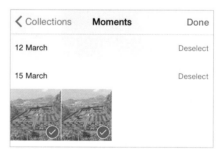

‹ Collections   **Moments**   Done
12 March   Deselect
15 March   Deselect

6 The selected items are added to the album (they stay in their original location, too)

‹ Albums   **Gardens**   Select

$+$

12 Practical Matters

This chapter looks at accessibility, security, and finding an iPhone.

Accessibility Issues

The iPhone tries to cater to as wide a range of users as possible, including those who have difficulty with vision, hearing, or physical and motor issues. There are a number of settings that can help with these areas. To access the range of Accessibility settings:

Don't forget

You will have to scroll down the page to view the full range of Accessibility options.

Hot tip

Drag the **On/Off Labels** button to **On** to show the relevant icons on the On/Off buttons.

1 Tap once on the **Settings** app

2 Tap once on the **General** tab

3 Tap once on the **Accessibility** link

4 The settings for **Vision**, **Interaction**, **Hearing**, **Media** and **Learning** are displayed here

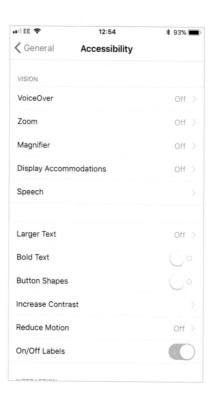

Vision settings

These can help anyone with impaired vision. There are options to hear items on the screen and also for making text easier to read:

1 Tap once on the **VoiceOver** link

VoiceOver	Off >

2 Drag this button to **On** to activate the VoiceOver function. This then enables items to be spoken when you tap on them

< Accessibility **VoiceOver**

VoiceOver

VoiceOver speaks items on the screen:
- Tap once to select an item
- Double-tap to activate the selected item
- Swipe three fingers to scroll

VoiceOver Practice

SPEAKING RATE

Speech >

Verbosity >

3 Select options for VoiceOver as required, such as speaking rate and pitch

4 Tap once on an item to select it (indicated by the black outline) and have it read out. Double-tap to activate a selected item or perform an action

< Accessibility **VoiceOver**

VoiceOver

VoiceOver speaks items on the screen:
- Tap once to select an item
- Double-tap to activate the selected item
- Swipe three fingers to scroll

Beware

VoiceOver works with the pre-installed iPhone apps and some apps from the App Store, but not all of them.

Don't forget

Another useful Accessibility function is **AssistiveTouch**, within the **Interaction** section. This offers a range of options for accessing items via tapping on the screen, rather than having to use swiping with two or more fingers. Tap once on this icon to access the items within AssistiveTouch after it has been turned **On**.

...cont'd

Zoom settings

Although the iPhone 8 and iPhone 8 Plus screens are among the largest in the smartphone market, there are times when it can be beneficial to increase the size of the items that are being viewed. This can be done with the Zoom feature. To use this:

1 Access the

Accessibility section as shown on page 178, and tap once on the Zoom link

2 By default, the **Zoom** button is **Off**

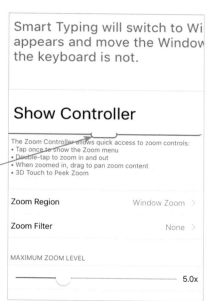

3 Drag the **Zoom** button to **On** to activate the Zoom window

4 Drag on this button to move the Zoom window around the current screen. Drag with three fingers within the Zoom window to move the screen area within it

Hot tip

Drag the **Show Controller** button to **On** in the Zoom settings to display a control button for the Zoom window. Tap once on the control button to view its menu of additional features, such as zooming in to greater or lesser amounts.

5 The Zoom window can also be used on the keyboard to increase the size of the keys. As in Step 4, drag with three fingers to move to other parts of the keyboard

Text size can also be increased within the Accessibility settings. To do this:

1 Under the **Vision** section, tap once on the **Larger Text** link

Larger Text	Off >

2 Drag the **Larger Accessibility Sizes** button **On** to enable compatible apps to show larger text sizes

3 Drag this slider to set the text size

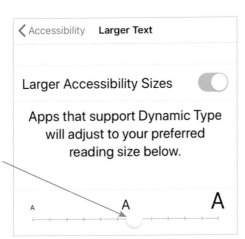

Beware

Not all apps support Dynamic Type for increasing text size, so the text in these apps will appear in their default sizes.

Setting Restrictions

Within the iPhone Settings app there are options for restricting types of content that can be viewed, and also actions that can be performed. These include:

- Turning off certain apps so that they cannot be used.

- Enabling changes to certain functions, so that only content that meets certain criteria can be accessed.

When setting restrictions, they can be locked so that no-one else can change them. To set and lock restrictions:

Hot tip

It is a good idea to set up some restrictions on your iPhone if young children and grandchildren are going to have access to it.

① Tap once on the **Settings** app

② Tap once on the **General** tab  General

③ Tap once on the **Restrictions** link

Restrictions

④ The restrictions are grayed-out; i.e. they have not been enabled for use yet

⑤ Tap once on the **Enable Restrictions** button

6 Type on the keypad to set a passcode for enabling and disabling restrictions (this is a four-digit code, as opposed to the six-digit one that can be used to lock and unlock the iPhone)

7 Re-enter the passcode

8 All of the Restrictions options become available. Drag these buttons **On** or **Off** to disable certain apps. If this is done, they will no longer be visible on the Home screen

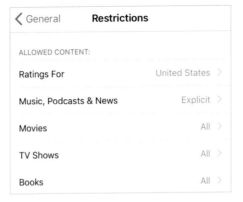

9 Tap once on the links under **Allowed Content** to specify restrictions for certain types of content, such as music, movies, books and apps

183

Beware

You can set restrictions for criteria such as age groups or explicit content. However, if you do this for specific individuals, such as grandchildren, explain to them what you have done, and why.

Finding Your iPhone

No-one likes to think the worst, but if your iPhone is lost or stolen, help is at hand. The Find My iPhone function (operated through the iCloud service) allows you to locate a lost iPhone, and send a message and an alert to it. You can also remotely lock it, or even wipe its contents. This gives added peace of mind, knowing that even if your iPhone is lost or stolen, its contents will not necessarily be compromised. To set up Find My iPhone:

Hot tip

Location Services and **Find My iPhone** both have to be turned **On** to enable this service. This can be done in the Settings app (**Settings > Privacy > Location Services > Find iPhone**, and under **Allow Location Access** tap once on **While Using the App**).

Hot tip

If you are using Family Sharing (see pages 58-61), you can use Find Friends to locate the devices of other Family Sharing members. This can be done from your online iCloud account, or with the Find Friends app.

1 Tap once on the **Settings** app and tap once on the Apple account ID button

2 Tap once on the **iCloud** tab

3 Tap once on the **Find My iPhone** link (if it is showing **Off**. If it is **On** then Find My iPhone is already activated)

4 Drag the **Find My iPhone** button to **On** to be able to find your iPhone on a map

Finding a lost iPhone

Once you have set up Find My iPhone, you can search for it through the iCloud service. To do this:

1 Log in to your iCloud account at **www. icloud.com** and tap once on the **Find iPhone** button (you also have to sign in again with your Apple ID)

2 Tap once on the **All Devices** button and select your iPhone. It is identified, and its current location is displayed on the map

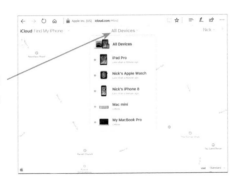

3 Tap once on the green circle to view details about when your iPhone was located

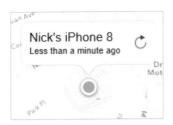

Nick's iPhone 8
Less than a minute ago

Don't forget

Click once on the **Erase iPhone** button to delete the iPhone's contents. This should be done as a last resort, if you think the contents may be compromised.

4 Tap once on the **Play Sound** button to send a sound alert to your iPhone

Nick's iPhone 8
Less than a minute ago

Play Sound   Lost Mode   Erase iPhone

5 Tap once on the **Lost Mode** button to lock your iPhone

6 Enter a six-figure passcode to lock the lost or stolen iPhone. The iPhone can now only be unlocked with this passcode

Cancel   Lost Mode

Lock this iPhone by entering a passcode.

● ● ● ● ● —

1	2 ABC	3 DEF
4 GHI	5 JKL	6 MNO
7 PQRS	8 TUV	9 WXYZ
Clear	0	⌫

Don't forget

If you have Apple Pay set up on your iPhone, this will be suspended if Lost Mode is enabled. It will be reactivated when the passcode is entered to unlock it and your Apple ID entered within Settings.

Avoiding Viruses

As far as security from viruses on the iPhone is concerned, there is good news and bad news:

- The good news is that, due to its architecture, most apps on the iPhone do not communicate with each other, unless specifically required to, such as the Mail and the Contacts apps. So, even if there were a virus, it would be difficult for it to infect the whole iPhone. Also, Apple performs rigorous tests on apps that are submitted to the App Store (although even this is not foolproof; see next bullet point).

- The bad news is that no computer system is immune from viruses and malware, and complacency is one of the biggest enemies of computer security. The iPhone's popularity means it is an attractive target for hackers and virus writers. There have been instances of photos in iCloud being accessed and hacked, but this was more to do with password security, or lack of, than viruses. Also, in September 2015 there was a malicious attack centered around the code used to create apps for the App Store. Although this was detected, some apps were affected before the virus was located and remedial action taken. This was known as the XcodeGhost attack, and was a reminder of the need for extreme vigilance against viruses and for users to check in the media for information about any new attacks.

Antivirus options

There are a few apps in the App Store that deal with antivirus issues, although not actually removing viruses. Two options to look at are:

- **McAfee** apps. The online security firm has a number of apps that cover issues such as privacy and passwords.

- **Norton** apps. Similar to McAfee, Norton offers a range of security apps for the iPhone.

Don't forget

Malware is short for malicious software, designed to harm your iPhone or access and distribute information from it.

Don't forget

Apple also checks apps that are provided through the App Store, and this process is very robust. This does not mean that it is impossible for a virus to infect the iPhone, so keep an eye on the Apple website to see if there are any details about iPhone viruses.

Index

191